Sculpture

Stanchion II, John Zeilman, American (1932-   )

a basic handbook
for students

Sculpture

Ronald L. Coleman
Bowling Green State University, Bowling Green, Ohio

WM. C. BROWN COMPANY PUBLISHERS, Dubuque, Iowa

Copyright © 1968 by
Wm. C. Brown Company Publishers

Library of Congress Catalog Card Number: 67-21317

ISBN 0—697—03330—9

Seventh Printing, 1974

Printed in the United States of America

FOREWORD

There is little justification for the spoken or written word in the visual arts except for technical direction. The qualities which make the visual arts unique have not been translated into a language. Those words which we do use are only indicative of value judgment or are dimensionally descriptive.

To demonstrate those elusive qualities of the arts requires more than words and is therefore beyond the capabilities of this writing. As a result, the bulk of the text is fundamentally a description of sculptural processes, with some notations concerning relationships occurring between sculpture and its culture.

Specifically, the text should prove of value to the young sculptor as an outline of fundamentals and processes. It was, of course, not designed to be — and never can be — a substitute for the experience of a teacher.

Notes to the Students

1. Always be a craftsman.
2. Solve each problem as quickly as possible. In the beginning a variety of experiences will be more valuable than ownership of a belabored student sculpture.
3. Work on more than one project at a time.
4. If an impasse is reached, put the work out of sight for some time. When again viewed, it may be seen in a new and revealing light.
5. Accept failure as normal. A failure is easier to analyze than a success. Study failures and learn from them. Failure is justified, if it results from an intelligent attempt to solve a particular problem, and is not thoughtlessly repeated.
6. Student works are primarily exercises; therefore, rarely is one so magnificent that it is too wonderful for the student to take a chance on improving it, even at the risk of complete failure.
7. Observe the work of others and learn from them.
8. Care for your tools. Use them as if they are extensions of your body and personality.
9. Sculpture is an arduous discipline. If the labor involved is too strenuous, seek another medium.
10. Be safety-conscious! Take protective measures before fatalities occur.

CONTENTS

PART ONE

The Essence of Sculpture

CHAPTER 1

Sculpture, which has been found among the earliest traces of all civilizations, has played an important part in the visual arts of most cultures. At times, as in the Golden Age of Greece, sculpture enjoyed the reputation of being the "Queen of the Arts."

With the revolt from academic restriction in the 19th century, the artist began to experiment with sculpture as he did with painting. He unleased new media and new tools and began to investigate the manipulation of space in a way forgotten since pre-classic times. Because of the odd characteristics of the human animal, every one of his cultures had had its own unique orientation. The ancient Egyptians oriented their culture around worship of the dead, and

The Estate

Figure 1. *Statuette of Min-nefer*, Egyptian, Late V. Dynasty, Limestone, The Cleveland Museum of Art, Purchase from the J. H. Wade Fund.

3

believed that the spirit would some day return to claim his long-preserved body. To protect against the eventuality that the body should be destroyed, the Egyptians required of their artists enduring statues and realistic portraits which would be recognized by the spirit when it returned to re-enter the body. It is to be expected, therefore, to find in the tombs of Egypt, many idealized full-length portraits of Egyptian royalty (Figure 1). On the other hand, during the same period, the people of the Mesopotamian valley did not believe in the preservation of the body; they believed instead that, rather than living for the future, it was necessary to live for the present. Their culture was oriented around life and its enjoyment, so their arts reflected this orientation by illustrating lion hunts, conquests, war parties, and the other business of an ancient royalty.

Each of the arts which is orientated to a culture is meaningful and functional within that orientation. The sculpture of the Egyptians would have had little meaning for the Mesopotamians and would probably not have been sculpturally functional for them. By the same token, the Egyptian, in considering the

sculpture of Mesopotamia, would probably have been blind to the cultural value of the objects, except in monetary terms.

THE REASONS FOR SCULPTURE

It is evident that when the nature of a culture changes for any reason, there will be a corresponding change in the art forms, if the art forms are to remain significant. Because of the advent of modern weapons, the creation of suits of armor like the one in Figure 2 is no longer a significant art form. A change in a culture often results in a change for the reason for the creation of works of art. Although it is futile to attempt to separate the reasons for the creation of works of art, we can generalize by saying that there are four primary reasons for the existence of any art form: the physical reasons, the intellectual reasons, the spiritual reasons, and the expressive reasons.

There are two ways in which sculpture may be desirable for its physical reasons: because of its mechanical properties, such as the sculptured doorknobs in Figure 3 or the doorplate in Figure 4, or because of its intrinsic properties (superior communication, either symbolically or psychologically). The intellectual reasons for sculpture involve the use of the abstract, perhaps for the purposes of analysis, interpretation, or prediction (Figure 5). The spiritual reasons are those which deal with the unprovable (areas of beliefs) such as religion or superstition

Figure 2. *Suit of armor in Maximilian style,* German, 16th century, The Cleveland Museum of Art, Gift of Mr. and Mrs. John L. Severance.

Figure 3. Door handles, Don Drumm, American (1935-), commissioned for a private home, cast aluminum.

Figure 4. Doorplate, Don Drumm, American (1935-), commissioned, cast aluminum.

(Figures 6 and 7). The expressive reasons are those which are a result of the emotional nature of man, and may include fear, pleasure, hate, and patriotism (Figure 8), to mention only a few.

The course of any art, in aligning itself with the orientation of a culture, is not a matter of happenstance. An art form and its contingent media will only evolve when there is a specific need (the function of the sculpture) and when the art form is contained within the physical, intellectual, and spiritual limits of the culture. A culture may require sculpture as evidence of its maturity or interest in "the cultural aspects of civilization"; it may require sculpture to serve in some form of therapy; or it may utilize sculpture as an advertising or politicking device. In any case, if the culture has no need of sculpture, none will develop. Although a culture may desire sculpture of a specific nature, the development of that sculpture may be denied or delayed because of the lack of physical means. It would have been difficult for the Egyptians to produce large, permanent, free-standing sculpture if large blocks of some enduring material like stone had not been available. If materials had been available, the Egyptians would still have needed the technology and the paraphernalia to produce the required kind of sculpture. It is obvious that sculpture cannot exist beyond the intellectual level of its culture. If either the concept or hypothesis is not within

Figure 6. *God the Father,* Johann Peter Schwanthaler the Elder (1720-1795), Austrian, painted and gilded wood, The Cleveland Museum of Art, Purchase from the J. H. Wade Fund.

Figure 5. *Family Group,* cast aluminum.

Figure 7. Primitive clay female figure.

Figure 9. *Lamp Bearer*, Delhi, India, cast metal, Collection of H. Hasselschwert.

Figure 8. *United States Marine Corps War Memorial,* "Marines Raising the American Flag On Iwo Jima," photo by courtesy of National Park Service, U. S. Department of the Interior.

the realm of a culture, there can be no basis for the production of sculpture within that concept or hypothesis. The development of sculpture is also limited by spiritual concepts. A culture which has a God as a structural basis for the explanation of its existence may evolve sculpture oriented towards the emulation or imitation of that God, but before sculpture can be oriented towards that emulation or imitation, the concept must exist. It is not necessary that the sculptor be convinced of the validity of the concept, but the concept must at least be part of his understanding of his culture.

Sculpture that is oriented to its culture is functional for the culture, in that the individuals within the culture are able to absorb the sculpture into their existence without conscious effort. The spoon is so well sculptured to fit the needs of our culture that only the details of the design of the device are questioned. The basic function is understood without effort by almost everyone. Other cultures, such as those in Africa or China, find the spoon somewhat foreign. When a sculptural form is well understood, that form may have great significance or meaning in relation to the culture. If, on the other hand, the sculpture is at odds with the culture, the sculpture will be meaningless, in which case man, rather than living through the sculpture, will live with the sculpture, perhaps assigning to it some temporary meaning or value. A hitching post like the one in Figure 10 is of little value to a man without a horse, unless he assigns to the device some quality other

Figure 10. Hitching post, American, cast iron.

than that of its intended function. The post could be placed for decoration, and if antique, some snob value could be attributed to it. The decorative value and the snob value have little significance to the culture except to display a skin of falseness on the culture, or to manifest the desire of the culture to retreat into the past. If the sculpture has no significance for a culture, man will live among such objects until he destroys them as he does old and "useless" buildings, or as did the "lime burners" of Rome who burned marble sculpture of the expired Greek civilization, in order to make cement.

Usually, the motives of the artist are so complex that no single predetermined reason can be given for the production of a work of art, and even then, the reasons for the continued existence of the sculpture may vary with time, geographical location, or numerous other factors. The artist who carves a figure of Christ in order to make a living, produces the sculpture for physical reasons, while the reason for its continued existence may be the spiritual reason of a congregation. The beginner almost invariably produces sculpture for physical reasons: because he is required by assignment to gain experience in the fundamentals of sculpture through the act of producing; and because he has not matured enough or had enough experience with life or with sculptural media to have something of significance to say of life with a sculptural medium. It is not until the creator has had a great deal of experience in life, that through his own growth, maturity, and perhaps curiosity, he will be able to create meaningful works of art, for other than superficial aspects of the reasons for producing sculpture. The artist must have a basis for

his creation, even if it is only the seeking of a new expression, new images, clarification of an ideal, a restatement of life, a search for universal truth, a method of communication, or a prediction (the attempt to free from rigid order). These things which the artist feels he must say are frequently answers to problems which have grown out of previous attempts to solve other problems. As the artist creates, new problems — and sometimes a variety of solutions — become obvious. Gradually the artist finds new areas unfolding for his investigation.

Young sculptors are frequently discouraged because they can find nothing worth producing or because they have no "ideas." They lack ideas because they have not had enough experience creating within the limits of their media. If the sculptor becomes thoroughly involved with his media, the media itself will suggest problems to be solved, and eventually some solutions to these problems. The artist should avoid the use of popular styles, fads, fashions, or gimmicks. The meaningfulness of sculpture, or any other art form, which relies on fashion for solution — like the silly statue of George Washington in a toga, influenced by a craze emulating the ancient Greeks (Figure 11), or like the deer in Figure 12 and the swan in Figure 13, which were either "cute" or novel — will be short-lived, because the success of the statuary will probably have resulted from their similarity to an accepted vogue rather than from the solution of a sculptural problem.

Figure 11. *George Washington*, Horatio Greenough, American (1805-1852), courtesy of the Smithsonian Institute, National Collection of Fine Arts.

Figure 12. *Deer*, painted cement novel 3-Dimensional object, American.

Figure 13. *Swan*, popular, but insignificant cement lawn planter, American.

THE LANGUAGE OF SCULPTURE

There are three languages of sculpture: the glyptic, the plastic, and the linear. The language of the sculptor is often determined by the medium that is readily available to him. If a putty-like medium is available, in all probability the plastic language will be utilized; if a resistant material such as stone is in ready supply, the language will more likely be glyptic; and if manageable wire is in easy access, the language will be linear — provided that in each case the other materials are less accessible.

Four techniques are utilized in the production of sculpture: manipulation, subtraction, substitution, and addition. Manipulation is considered primarily a technique of the plastic language, subtraction a technique of the glyptic language, and substitution and addition techniques of all three languages. Of course these sculptural languages are visual not mechanical languages; therefore, it is not unlikely that stone (which is usually associated with the glyptic language) may be carved in such a way as to become plastic in appearance.

The glyptic language is that which emphasizes the material from which the sculpture is being created, whether the material is stone, bronze, or clay. Not only does glyptic sculpture retain the characteristics of the medium, but it usually retains basic geometric qualities of the mass from which it is produced, as in Figure 14. Frequently, because of the inherent formality of this language, figures created in this manner face forward — static, without twist to the body, as if the body were part of the grain of the medium. This convention, illustrated in Figures 15 and 16, is known as the "law of frontality." Glyptic sculpture retains the tactile, color, and tensile qualities of the material from which it was produced.

Figure 14. *Torso of a Female Deity*, Cambodian, classic Khmer period, about 12th century, The Toledo Museum of Art, Gift of Edward Drummond Libbey.

Figure 15. Contemporary wood carving, stained black, Tanganyika.

Figure 17. Ceramic Mask, contemporary.

Figure 16. Contemporary wood carving, stained black, Tanganyika.

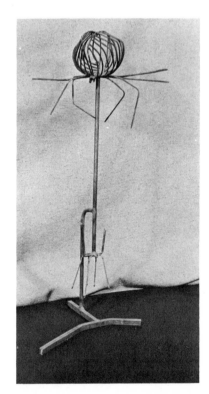

Figure 18. Spider, welded iron.

Plastic sculpture is fluid or malleable in nature, because of the fluidity or malleability of the media from which it is produced, or because of the fluidity of the subject with which it deals. Pliable media, like clay or wax, are pushed, modeled, and squeezed until they take on the flowing characteristics of the subject, as in Figure 17. Plastic media have great immediacy and are autographic and intimate, while glyptic media are resistant, impersonal, and formal. Unlike the rigid figures produced in the glyptic lan-guage, plastic sculpture possesses some degree of action or movement.

Although it has ancient origins, linear sculpture is only beginning to mature as a language. Since the advent of gas and electric welding, the artist has been able to assemble wire to enfold space in a line-like substance, like the spider in Figure 18, resulting in a light, airy, stringy quality which cannot be obtained in either the massiveness of the glyptic or the fluidity of the plastic sculptural languages.

THE METHODS OF EXPRESSION

In each of the languages, the artist is able to utilize five methods of expression: the realistic, the naturalistic, the impressionistic, the expressionistic, and the abstract. In the realistic style, the artist observes, interprets, generalizes, simplifies, rearranges, and elaborates on what he sees in nature. Invariably the finished product is easily recognized as an object typical of its kind, but not as a specific one of a kind. The face on the head in Figure 19 is a general face, not a particular or specific face, and is therefore, realism.

Naturalistic sculpture results when the artist attempts to eliminate all editorializing in order to imitate an object as faithfully as possible. As in the bust of Coypel (Figure 20), every detail, no matter how insignificant, is copied, whether that detail is beneficial to the overall sculpture or not. Naturalistic sculpture is of a specific object and, because of its extreme detail, cannot represent but can only mimic. It is this characteristic which makes debatable the validity of naturalism as an art form.

Impressionistic sculpture is that which possesses only a vague visual semblance of a subject, thereby allowing the observer to interpret what he sees (Figures 21 and 22). The image discovered by the observer is not as dependent on the actual shape of the sculpture or on the surface texture, as it is on the way the light and, therefore, the shadows fall on the apparently spontaneous undulations and convolutions of the medium, to give the general impression of the subject. Impressionistic sculpture is not profuse with finished detail, but has hints at detail which facilitate the inclusion of detail by the observer.

Figure 19. *Head,* student work, cast bronze.

Figure 20. *The Painter, Noel Nicolas Coypel,* by Jean Baptiste Lemoyne (1704-1778), French, The Toledo Museum of Art, Gift of Edward Drummond Libbey.

Figure 21. *Horse,* student work, plaster.

Figure 22. *Eve*, Auguste Rodin (1840-1917), French, The Toledo Museum of Art, Gift of Edward Drummond Libbey.

probable that no sculpture is one pure method of expression. It is obvious for instance, that even the illusionistic naturalism is greatly abstracted from nature.

Figure 23. *Singing Man,* Ernst Barlach (1870-1938), German, bronze, The Cleveland Museum of Art, Hinman B. Hurlbut Collection.

Expressionistic sculpture is that which is based on the artist's moods, opinions, and emotions, so that there is inherent or implied emotion, usually related to ideas or movement — and at times to value or subject, as in Barlach's introverted *Singing Man* (Figure 23).

Abstract sculpture, to some degree, includes all sculpture, because the initial conversion from nature to the inanimate is probably the greatest abstraction of all. But technically only that sculpture which has its origin in nature and, like realism, is a result of interpretation, generalization, simplification, rearrangement, and elaboration, is known as abstract. Unlike realism, abstraction may involve the processes of simplification, rearrangement, or elaboration to such an extent that the original device, image, or source of inspiration is no longer recognizable, as in the sculpture by Henry Moore (Figure 24). More general definitions of abstraction include art which does not have recognizable, visually logical subject matter.

It is entirely possible that to some extent each of the languages could be created in each of the methods of expression, but each language seems to some degree to be suited to particular technical methods. Glypticism, for instance, is better suited to realism than naturalism, because in an attempt to capture detail in naturalism, the quality of the material (necessary to glypticism) would be lost. It is also

Figure 24. *Reclining Figure,* Henry Moore (1898-   ), English, The Toledo Museum of Art, Gift of Edward Drummond Libbey.

THE BASICS OF SCULPTURE

There are three components of sculpture: form, content, and subject matter. All three of these components are dependent on and related to each other, but since the emphasis put on the component is to some extent culturally controlled, the components are not equal in importance. Form is the order or unity which comes from the use of the elements of sculpture (shape, value, space, line, time, texture, and color), and is the result of physical manipulation of the elements — and the relationships caused by that manipulation. Content, the source of which is form, is the meaning or significance of a work of art which manifests itself in aesthetic experience. Subject matter is the theme or story that is represented in a work, and is the only component independent of the others, but when subject matter is used independently of the other components, the result will not be an art form. Subject matter which reflects material things is object-oriented, while subject matter which is concerned with the abstract is concept-oriented.

If it were necessary to arrange the elements of sculpture in order of importance, shape would probably be the first in place. Shape is a generally measurable area, enclosed by contour — caused by line, contrasting color, texture, or value. In sculpture, except for surface embellishment, visible shape usually depends on the position of the viewer and the direction of the source of illumination. Movement around the sculpture results in the change of the appearance of various shapes within the sculpture because the contours of many of the shapes are simply the edges of curved surfaces which appear or disappear as the viewer changes positions. The same is true of the shapes formed by illumination: as the light source changes direction (as the sun changes its position), the shapes formed by shadows change (Figures 25A, 25B, and 25C). It is not necessary for the shapes to be of solid material. An opening surrounded by finite material, such as a hole in a block of stone, forms an area known as a void, which, like tangible material, can have shape (Figures 26 and 27). When the implied enclosure of space is the goal of the artist, as in much linear sculpture, the defining material is subordinate to the dominative void. On the other hand, the mass of most glyptic sculpture is dominant, and resultant voids, if any, are subordinate.

Shape within a piece of sculpture is capable of creating the emotional structure of the sculpture. Shape, as it is formed through three dimensions, blocks the passage of light, creating shadow-value patterns, which if small, frequent, and angular, will

Figure 25A. Light source from the left.

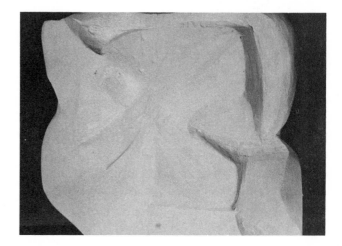

Figure 25B. Light source from the center.

Figure 25C. Light source from the right.

Figure 26. Void in stone.

Figure 28. Laminated wood, student work.

Figure 27. Voids in stone.

Figure 29. Simulated stone.

appear excited (Figure 28); or if the patterns are
large, and curvilinear, will appear calm (Figure 29).
Careful manipulation of shape can give an appearance to sculpture, often desired, known as monumentality (Figure 30). An object is monumental when it
appears to be larger than life size, or when it can be

Figure 30. *Cast Aluminum Bronze Monument,* approxi-
mately 5 inches high.

produced in any size without visually disturbing effects. The most effective size of a piece of sculpture is generally dictated by its detail, textural effects, or shape character.

Value is the element which permits most sculpture to be visually understood. Value is that quality of light (of any hue) which ranges from light to dark, and which results from the absorbtion or reflection of light by a surface. Rather than depending only on pigmentation for value range, as in the graphic arts, the sculptor also depends on the presence or absence of light — the lighted surface or the shadowed surface — to establish form (Figures 31, 32, and 33). Shadow is so important to the sculptor that frequently the shape and texture of the sculpture are distorted to make the shadow on the surface of a sculpture visually effective. It should be noted that, for the most part in sculptural media, it is value which describes all of the other elements except time.

The differentiating element between the two-dimensional and three-dimensional arts is space. The illusion of space which is achieved in the graphic arts is not a manipulatable device, but instead is a trick of the eye or mind, resulting from the manipulation of the other elements; therefore, space cannot be considered to be one of the elements of graphics. In the three-dimensional arts, however, space is one of the usable devices of the art. The illusion resulting from the use of perspective in graphic art can be used in re-

Figure 32. Cast plaster, student work.

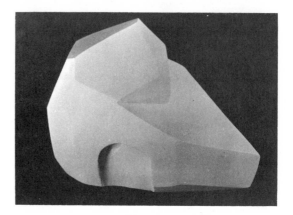

Figure 33. Cast plaster, student work.

lief sculpture to distort natural space in such a way as to lend the appearance of greater depth than actually exists in the sculpture. Because pure space has no visual qualities, a medium is required to demonstrate its existence and to delineate the boundaries of the space which the sculptor desires to utilize.

Except for intaglio relief, such as that of the ancient Egyptians (Figure 74), there was little purely linear sculpture until the advent of welded metal and the common use of wire. Now, as illustrated in Figures 34, 35, 36, and 67, linear sculpture is becoming commonplace. Unlike the line of graphic media — which is easily produced and, therefore, highly autographic — sculptural line is difficult to produce and tends to be highly formal (Figure 37). This is especially true when the line is dependent on the intersection of planes as it is in Figures 32 and 33; contours, as in Figure 36; textural limits, or the linear quality of wire, as in Figure 37 (monotonous because of its consistent thickness). Line quality can be controlled to a great extent when it is carved in soft clay, but this approaches drawing and tends to become two-dimen-

Figure 31. Primitive ceramic clay pot.

sional. It wasn't until the technique of shaping wire through welding became prevalent that, by modifying the wire, the sculptor was able to establish significant expressive quality in a three-dimensional linear medium.

Line has the ability to create movement and direction across surface and around the bulk of a piece of

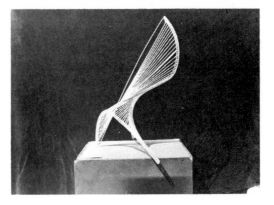

Figure 37. Student work, aluminum rod and string.

Figure 34. *Boy on a Bicycle,* student work, iron wire.

sculpture. Because "line" does not actually exist in nature and is, in reality, an invention of the artist, the word "edge" (a more defining but less inclusive term) is often used, particularly in relation to mass, plane, or contour.

Time is probably the least understood of all the elements. It has two sources: one in the nature of the viewer, the other in the nature of the sculpture. Time resulting from the nature of the viewer is almost completely beyond the control of the artist, and is the amount of time that the viewer uses to observe areas of the sculpture, or the time it takes to move around a piece of sculpture in an effort to study the entire composition. The artist, in causing a work to be interesting, may thereby cause the viewer to utilize more time in the study of the work, but the artist is not able to significantly control the amount of time involved (Figure 38).

Figure 35. *The Politician,* welded iron rod.

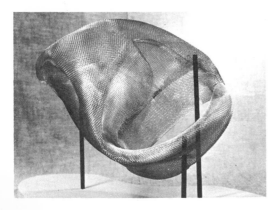

Figure 36. Student work, wire screen.

Figure 38. Both objects have similar profiles (contours), but the left sculptural object requires more time for visual inspection than the graphic right object.

The source of time resulting from the nature of the sculpture is subject to a great deal of control by the artist. This is the time required by the object to complete mobility within itself. Such sculpture is designed so that physical change takes place mechanically (Figures 39 and 40). Except for random change, the total time required for all of the changes to take place is designed into the sculpture by the artist. Spring motors or electrically driven figures are devices that depend on the artist's utilization of the element of time.

Texture is that tactile quality of a surface which affects both the sense of touch and the sense of sight. There are two primary sources of texture in sculpture: that which is indigenous to the medium (Figure 41) and that which the artist produces on the surface of the sculpture in addition to, or in spite of, the natural texture of the material (Figures 42, 43, and 44). In sculpture all textures are actual except those resulting from color or value patterns which are part of the pigmentation of the medium, such as the grain in marble or wood (Figures 45 and 46). In order to make a work effective, the artist sometimes simulates textures by copying from other surfaces such as skin or hair (Figure 20), or he may create abstract textures (Figures 47 and 48) by reorganizing or simplifying other textures.

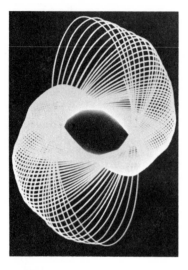

Figure 39. Track made by mechanical movement of a mobile.

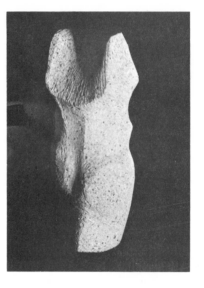

Figure 41. Texture resulting from mica flakes in cement aggregate.

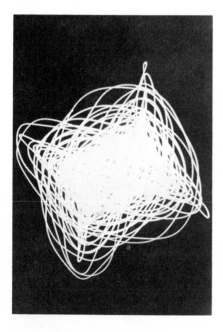

Figure 40. Track made by mechanical movement of a mobile.

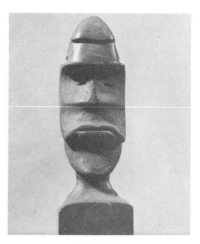

Figure 42. Texture caused by tool marks in walnut.

Figure 43. Texture resulting from form in cast aluminum.

Figure 46. Indigenous texture resulting from grain in rosewood.

Figure 44. Mechanical texture and texture resulting from form.

Figure 47. Abstract texture used to indicate hair. Primitive figure in volcanic stone.

Figure 45. Indigenous texture resulting from grain in walnut.

Figure 48. Impressed abstract texture in ceramic clay.

Color is as natural to sculpture as it is to the graphic arts, but the manipulation and control of color, for the most part, differs greatly between the two media. While some wood and metal sculpture is painted and ceramic sculpture can be glazed in every hue of the rainbow (Figures 49 and 50), the color of most sculpture is a direct result of the use of its medium. Woods, stones, clays, and metals are found having colors ranging from white through gray to black, and include reds, purples, blues, greens, yellows, and oranges. The natural color of a medium is usually preferred to applied color, because color that is applied to a surface tends to hide the innate qualities of the grain (along with some of the detail), which contribute to the desirability of the medium, and because the spacial effect resulting from the proximity of dissimilar colors often come into conflict with the actual space involved in the sculpture, causing visual confusion. By painting a shadowed area white and a lighted area black, an illusion can be created which would reverse normal visual space.

Figure 49. *Mouse*, N. Coleman, American (1936-   ), ceramic clay with white and brown mat glaze.

Figure 50. Painted primitive jug, ceramic clay.

THE PRINCIPLES OF ORDER

In order to distill meaning from form, the artist regiments his elements in such a way that some understandable organization, or some order, is achieved. In his arranging, he utilizes the Principles of Order: he considers balance, harmony, variety, economy, proportion, and movement, each in relation to the other.

Balance is used in two ways — in relation to weight or gravity, and in relation to the other Principles of Order and the elements. Gravitational balance can be divided into two pure types: radial balance and asymmetrical balance.

There are, of course, various mixtures and degrees of the two e.g., monosymmetrical balance and approximate symmetry. Pure radial balance exists only in a perfect sphere. No matter which way a plane passes through the sphere, so long as the plane passes through the center, the resulting divisions on each side of the plane will be identical, measurably balanced. Asymmetrical balance is a "personal" balance which depends on "unlikes" of equal importance, as in the mobile shown in Figure 70. There will generally be agreement between individuals, but because of physiological and psychological differences, no two individuals will see alike; therefore, what one individual interprets as satisfactory balance may be interpreted as imbalance by some other person. Asymmetrical balance seldom has a definite fulcrum or dividing line. Monosymmetry is a mixture of radial and asymmetrical balance; it has only one dividing axis (usually vertical), with opposite sides equal (Figure 51). Approximate symmetry, on the other hand, utilizes a general dividing line, with opposite sides similar but not identical (Figure 52).

Balance in relation to the Principles of Order and the element is balance which depends on psychological tensions which are sensed by the observer between the elements and harmony, variety, economy, movement, and proportion. Like asymmetrical balance, it is "personal," and depends on the sensitivity and personality of the observer.

As the artist has a small degree of control over the observer through the use of these tensions, he can cause the beholder to sense anger, excitement, melancholia, sadness, and so on. By using great economy and harmony, the artist can create a still, simple, dignified sculpture (Figure 53); or by using much movement and great variety, he can create violently florid sculpture (Figure 54). The presence of tensions in the organization of the sculpture results in characteristics known as harmony and variety. Harmony is the result of the use of elements in such a

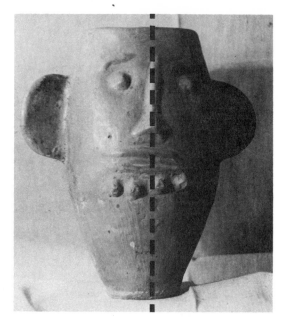

Figure 53. *Seated Nude*, Aristide Maillol (1861-1944), French, The Toledo Museum of Art, Gift of Edward Drummond Libbey.

Figure 51. Bisymmetry, primitive ceramic clay jug.

Figure 52. *Tara*, Nepal, India, 20th century, cast metal, Collection of H. Hasselschwert.

Figure 54. *Sextus Tarquinius Threatening Lucrece*, Hubert Gerhard, German, The Cleveland Museum of Art, Purchase from the J. H. Wade Fund.

Figure 55. *Celtic Head,* about 3rd century, England, The Cleveland Museum of Art, Gift of Dr. and Mrs. Jacob Hirsch.

Figure 57. Harmony through rhythm.

Figure 58. Harmony.

Figure 56. *Terminal of a Balustrade,* Cambodian, classic Khmer period, 10th century, The Toledo Museum of Art, Gift of Edward Drummond Libbey.

way that there is conformity among the parts (Figure 55). If similarity (repetition) is utilized in a manner which can be predicted (having a uniform procedure similar to a musical beat), the composition has rhythm (Figure 56). Rhythm which can be easily and entirely predicted becomes monotonous. Harmony relieved of this tendency toward monotony by change (variety) is shown in Figures 57 and 58. Rhythms which are dull can be made interesting by selectively emphasizing parts of the rhythm in such a way as to complicate the beat-forming rhythms within the rhythm (Figure 59). When some part of a rhythm is emphasized in such a way as to surprise the viewer, the rhythm is said to be syncopated.

Variety is dissimilarity of parts and is achieved by utilizing parts of contrasting or opposing natures (Figure 60), or by elaborating on parts until their complexity competes, or contrasts, with other more simple parts. The artist's point of balance between harmony and variety determines, to a great extent, the dynamic or static quality of a piece of sculpture. Variety carried to extremes becomes chaos!

Figure 61. *Water Buffalo,* lamp, India, glazed ceramic clay.

Figure 62. *Design Problem #1,* student work, wood.

Figure 59. Rhythms formed within rhythms.

Figure 60. Variety through dissimilarity of parts.

A work of art can become far too complex to allow the reason for its existence to be evident. The artist finds that it is necessary to eliminate or sacrifice material or detail of lesser importance, in order that the composition not be obscured in a mass of irrelevant material. Great economy results in abstraction. The purpose of economy is to achieve the maximum effect with the simplest design, like the beautifully simple *Water Buffalo* in Figure 61.

There are two kinds of movement found in sculpture, that which is implied within the object (Figure 62) and real motion (Figures 39, 40, and 69). Implied movement tends to draw the various parts of the composition together — the greater the similarity and proximity between the parts, the greater the tension, and the more rapid or direct the motion. Real motion, on the other hand, as was discussed under the element "time," describes the totality of the sculpture rather than the surface movement.

Proportion is part-to-part relationships in terms of size. It, like asymmetrical balance, requires judgment, and is therefore a personal matter. When proportion is concerned with the relationship of the parts to the total sculpture, or the total sculpture to its surroundings, it is then known as "scale."

CHAPTER 2

The Concepts of Sculptural Entity

SCULPTURE-IN-THE-ROUND

There are two concepts of sculptural entity: sculpture-in-the-round (free-standing sculpture), as in Figure 63, and relief sculpture (Figure 64). Sculpture that has been manipulated on at least four sides is known as sculpture-in-the-round, and can be achieved in four ways: monolithic totality, totality through volume (by planes or lines), totality through multiple units (two or more similar or dissimilar units), and totality through real or implied motion.

Monolithic totality is a solid (dense) unit, usually —though not always—a geometric mass, such as a quarried stone, a block of wood, or even a solid block of bronze.

Totality through volume occurs either as a construction of planes such as in the lamp shade of folded paper illustrated in Figure 66 or as in a suit of armor formed of sheets of metal (Figure 2), or as a construction of line, as in the structure of a wire bird cage, in which the surface is not continuous, but is still spacially limiting.

Figure 63. Free standing ceramic clay figure, primitive.

Figure 64. Growth plate, cast aluminum

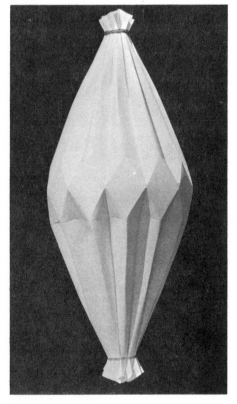

Figure 65. *Mary and Joseph,* Harold Hasselschwert, American (1930-   ), sheet metal.

Figure 66. Folded paper shape.

Figure 67. *Dingle-Dangle,* Don Drumm, American (1935-   ), moving sculpture with noise attachments, welded steel.

Totality through multiple units can easily be compared to a bunch of grapes, the overall cluster being composed of small units; or totality through multiple units can be compared to the total human body, which is composed of a series of connected cylinders, cones, spheres, and so on. Each unit may have a specific shape; the unit and its shape is subordinate to the overall structure.

Totality through real or implied motion is dependent on the movement, or indicated (potential) movement, of a filament of the sculpture through space — in such a way that the moving filament utilizes greater area than the same filament occupies when standing still. A child's top while spinning does not occupy greater space than when it is standing still, nor does

Figure 68. *White Loops and Red Spiral on Black,* stabile-mobile, Alexander Calder, American 1898-   ), The Cleveland Museum of Art, Gift of The Halle Bros. Co.

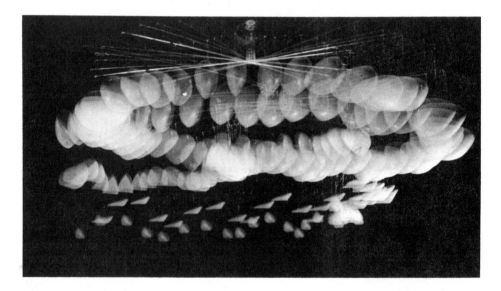

Figure 69.

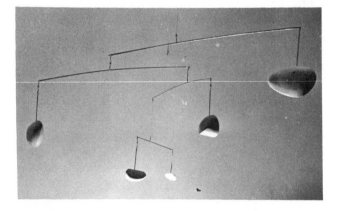

Figure 70.

its movement result in a change of shape, but the same is not true of a fan blade. The blade has one shape and occupies a given amount of space when motionless, but as a totality, it occupies greater space and has a different shape while it is spinning. This principle is used in mobiles, as in Figure 68, when many possible movements are designed for the filaments. The wires and attached plates, which are the filaments, occupy greater space — both visually and physically — when they are in motion (Figure 69) than when they are at rest (Figure 70). This motion does not have to be accomplished to create the image of the probable limits of the totality; it need only be implied by line, shape, or one of the other elements.

RELIEF SCULPTURE

Totality is not achieved in relief sculpture in the same way that it is in sculpture-in-the-round. Because relief sculpture is shallow manipulation on one plane, it is viewed only from the front; it is usually obvious that the surface does not continue behind the relief, but instead flows onto or into the background or supporting surface. Unlike sculpture-in-the-round, relief form defies definition as a pure sculptural totality; in that the object is modeled from a surface, deep space is not involved. Renoir's *Judgment of Paris* (Figure 71), illustrates that only minor convolutions or undulations in a surface are needed to give the illusion of mass or volume.

There are two kinds of relief sculpture: intaglio relief and cameo relief. Intaglio relief is divided into two styles: the first is a simple line carved into the surface of the material — in effect, a contour drawing — as in Figure 73; the second kind of intaglio relief is a depression carved into the surface of the medium,

Figure 71. *Judgment of Paris,* Pierre Auguste Renoir, French, 20th century, bronze, The Cleveland Museum of Art, Purchase from the J. H. Wade Fund.

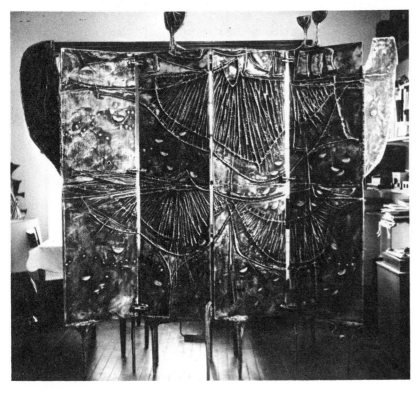

Figure 72. Folding aluminum screen, Don Drumm, American (1935-   ), cast and welded aluminum.

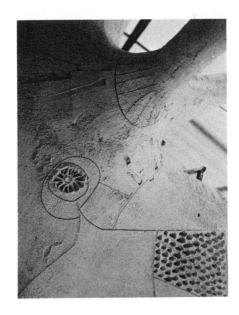

Figure 73. *Detail of a support column,* Don Drumm, American (1935-   ), from a stairwell in a private home, plaster.

permitting the background to stand high and leaving the design concave (bowl-like) in the surface, as in Figure 74.

Cameo relief is the exact reverse of intaglio. Rather than cutting the design away, or incising a drawn line into a surface, the modeled object is left standing out, hill-like, from the surface, (Figure 75). Occasionally the entire background is not carved away to the full depth of the figures, but the figures still stand out from their immediate surroundings. Because of the highly restricting nature of relief sculpture and because of the lack of definable mass, relief sculpture is often held akin to two-dimensional design, in which the artist relies on shadow, rather than pigment, for value relationship.

Figure 74. *Nobleman in Sacerdotal Vestments, Adoring,* Egyptian, Early XXVI Dynasty, The Cleveland Museum of Art, Gift of the Hanna Fund.

Figure 75. *Madonna and Child,* Antonio Rossellino, Italian (1427-1478), The Toledo Museum of Art, Gift of Edward Drummond Libbey.

PART TWO

The Technical Methods

CHAPTER 3

Introduction to the Technical Methods

The availability of a medium and the desirability of its qualities lead to the development of a philosophy which attempts to interrelate the medium and man's culture. Consequently, a philosophic controversy has existed over the appropriateness, validity, or superiority of the subtractive technique as opposed to the manipulative technique. These two methods evolved because of the abundance of both stone (a resistant, somewhat permanent material) and clay (a plastic, fragile material). The controversy itself is of little consequence, as the quality of a work of art depends only partially on the kind of technique or method involved in the production of the art form. The only note of importance here is that the controversy emphasized the relation of a medium to the methods to which it is best suited and demonstrates that, as far as man is concerned, all media are not equally suited, psychologically or physiologically, to every technique. Stone is hardly a material that can be squeezed into shape by hand; instead, it must be chipped or carved laboriously and slowly to its proper form; therefore, stone does not lend itself to immediate, spontaneous expression. Clay, on the other hand, is highly autographic and fluid, to such an extent that it responds easily to the touch. It would seem, then, that clay would be suited to an emotional, spontaneous process instead of to a pondering, intellectual, incubation-like process. Naturally, some media are versatile and, like clay, can be exploited in more than one technique.

There are four primary technical methods of producing three-dimensional objects: manipulation, subtraction, addition, and substitution, each of which is discussed in following chapters. It must be noted that much sculpture is produced by combinations of the four technical methods, some of which are included in the text.

Because they require a fairly advanced technology, the techniques of addition (build up) and substitution (casting) occur later in history than manipulation and subtraction. Both of these complex techniques were used in imitation of the simpler techniques, until a point was reached at which the integrity of the techniques became subverted.

The additive technique is often used as a substitute for carved stone or as a pattern for casting; in each, the natural qualities of the additive medium are destroyed in imitating a cast or poured material. The finished product usually looks like a cheap copy or worse.

The manipulative technique suffers the same illness that affects the additive technique. When a manipulative medium such as clay is reproduced by being cast (perhaps in bronze, for purposes of preservation), the result is a secondhand bronze imitation of a clay model. If clay is modeled to suit the nature of flowing metal, the clay medium is perverted, and the result is a bronze imitation of a clay imitation of cast bronze. Fortunately, since the translation from one material to another is difficult, and the differences "seem" slight, we have been able to accept the technique of substitution in spite of these disadvantages.

CHAPTER 4

Manipulation

The manipulative technique known as modeling requires a medium which is pliable or can be made pliable during the period in which it is being modeled. It must be able to maintain its shape and support most of its own weight. Manipulative media in common use today include clay, wax, plastic, and metal. Media which are highly plastic require the use of armatures to support the bulk of the material. Armature material can also be used as core material to displace a large bulk of the medium — for reasons of economy, in the case of an expensive medium, or to save weight.

Armature material used in the manipulative technique include soft aluminum clothesline wire, heavy lead-coated electrical wire, heavy galvanized iron wire, copper pipe, galvanized iron pipe, iron rods, wood lath (for trellised armatures), and expanded metal such as plaster lath (for large relief sculpture). Clay sculpture which is to be fired can be modeled over a core of tightly bundled and tied excelsior, cloth, or paper. Because clay shrinks as it dries and as it is fired, the armature should be compressible enough to allow the clay to shrink without cracking; it should also be combustible so that the armature material will burn away during the firing process.

Additional armature materials available for other techniques include metal screen, styrofoam, inflatable materials such as balloons or preshaped sheet plastic bags, and combinations of any of these materials.

Armature material which is corrosive or can be destroyed by the media should be shellacked or lacquered to prevent direct contact with the media. Iron should be shellacked to prevent rusting, and styrofoam should be treated with an impervious coating if it is to be covered with solvent plastics.

Wire armatures are bent to shape to form the "bone structure" of the sculpture, then fastened to a temporary base, such as a thick slab of wood (Figure 76). If the medium is especially soft as some clays are, it may be necessary to wire small blocks of wood to the armature to prevent the wire from pulling through the clay, allowing the clay to drop off of the armature.

Copper or iron pipe armature can be threaded and fitted together in almost any desired form (Figure 77). Copper tubing is easily soldered, and the soft grade can be bent to shape without the application of heat. The hard grade of copper tubing requires heating in the area of the desired bend before the pipe can be readily bent. Joints to be soldered should be first cleaned with sandpaper, then coated with a soldering paste such as "Nokorode." Solder (the common wire variety without a flux core) will then flow around the heated joint by capillary action, forming a firm bond when cool. Heat can be applied with large soldering irons, but a far more efficient tool is a Bernz-a-Matic-type torch.

Iron pipe, iron rods, and heavy iron wire can be welded and bent to shape with the application of heat, as in the case of the hard copper tubing. Gal-

vanized iron pipe is not safe to weld under normal conditions, as the zinc fumes given off as a white gas during the welding process are quite toxic. Symptoms of zinc poisoning are dizziness, severe headache, sore eyes, and nausea; in general, symptoms closely resemble those of the flu. Mild cases seldom last more than 24 hours.

Large armatures can be constructed of wood framing, over which wood lath or plaster lath is nailed to form a surface for the medium. Wood lath is often used for huge ceramic relief sculpture.

Soft armature materials such as excelsior, paper, or cloth can be bundled and tied with string or wire (Figures 78, 79, and 80) and, if necessary, treated with a waterproofer to form a core for a medium. Because of the flexible nature of these armatures, they are primarily used for small sculpture.

Figure 76.

Figure 78.

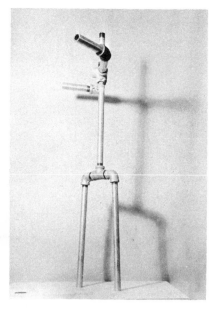

Figure 77.

Figure 79.

Figure 80.

Expanded metals are quite flexible and can be shaped, cut, and joined easily. Because of these characteristics the metal can be cut into patterns or shapes, formed three-dimensionally, and wired together with black iron wire to create a shell, the same shape and almost the same size as the finished sculpture (Figures 81, 82, and 83). All that remains is to isolate the armature and apply the medium. Expanded metal is so controllable that it is considered normal to design the armature so that only one-quarter inch of medium need be applied to complete the sculpture.

Figure 82.

Figure 81.

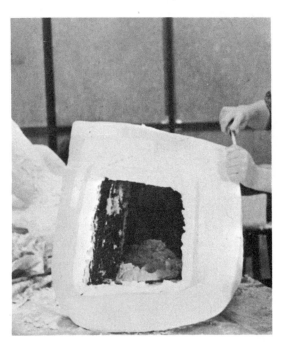

Figure 83.

34

Styrofoam is available in logs of almost any size. The common blocks (2″ × 24″ × 96″ and 4″ × 18″ × 120″) are available in many lumber yards as insulation or flotation material for dock construction. It is easily cut with a grapefruit knife (Figure 84), saw, router bit (Figure 85), or hot wire Figure (86), * and can be joined with stiff wire, wooden pins, or Elmer's Glue, some contact cements, collodion, or styrofoam cement. Glue which dissolves or softens styrofoam should be avoided.

Inflatable materials such as balloons or plastic bags shaped by the thermowelding process can also be used for armatures, but the machinery for welding plastic is not readily available — which makes the extensive use of plastic somewhat impractical for this purpose. Inflated balloons are simply joined with tape, string, or contact cement, and then covered with the desired medium.

Figure 84.

Figure 85.

*Refer to page 122 for diagram showing the construction of a hot wire cutter.

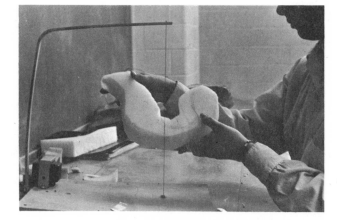

Figure 86.

Most armature materials can be combined. Probably the most used combination is wire and plaster-soaked burlap or cheese cloth, as in Figures 87 - 90. Iron rod or pipe is also frequently used with expanded metal.

It is vital that the armature be properly formed, as the armature is the foundation around which the sculpture is constructed. Proportions and directions of movement must be absolutely correct in the armature, or the sculpture will not be correctly proportioned or shaped. In some cases, parts of the medium can be removed to reveal the armature so that it can be adjusted, but this kind of wasted time and effort can be eliminated by correct armature design. It is also important to consider the armature as a core around which the medium is to be wrapped. Space must therefore be provided for the medium all around each part of the armature, as well as where one part of the armature nears another; otherwise, parts of the sculpture will be buried in the medium (Figure 91).

Figure 87.

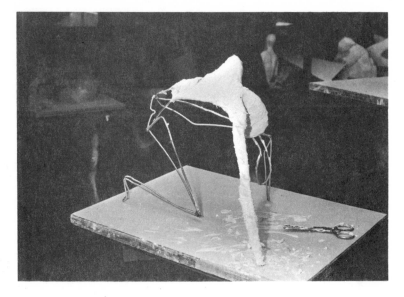

Figure 88.

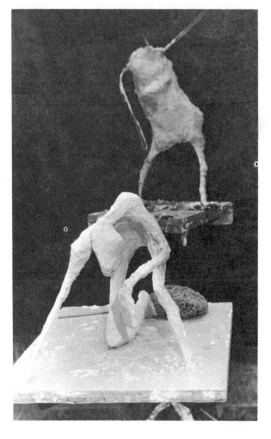

Figure 90.

Figure 89.

Figure 91. If sufficient space is not provided between the arm and the leg, the arm will become buried in the process of building up the leg.

Figure 92. Ceramic clay bowl, Ohio Mound Builder.

Figure 93. *Head,* ceramic clay.

CLAY

Water-base modeling clay can be obtained pre-mixed, wet, and ready to use, but clay purchased this way is very expensive. It is usually purchased in a dry air-floated powder state, and is prepared by sifting the powder into water, and permitting it to soak (slake) until the water is absorbed into the clay and a thick, putty-like consistency is obtained. If the clay is to be used for ceramics, it is sifted into water until a thick but fluid slip is formed, allowed to age a day or so, and then is mixed with a power mixer if possible (blunged). Excess water is removed by evaporation or by pouring the slip onto dry absorbent plaster slabs known as bats. Once the clay has dried to a proper plasticity, it is stored in crocks, garbage cans, plastic bags, or other nonabsorbent, airtight containers in order to preserve its moisture content until it is used. The water in clay may have a tendency to settle, so it may be necessary to turn the clay occasionally to prevent the bottom from becoming mucky and the top from getting too hard. If the clay stiffens too much to be used, additional water can be added to soften it. If

clay is required in large quantities, it should be prepared mechanically, in a filter press, a pug mill, or a muller.

Water-base clay is inexpensive, can be washed away with water, is responsive to tools, and many of these clays can be used as a ceramic body. They have some disadvantages: all are not suited to modeling, in that they may be too coarse, too gummy, or too slimy; they require preparation and constant care; and may tend to crack, warp, or shrink as they harden. Water-base clay hardens if not deliberately kept wet while being worked.

Oil-base clays (plasteline, plastecine, and plastilina) are modeling media which use nondrying oils such as glycerine, lanolin or even plastic, instead of water to make the clay or talc mass plastic. They are purchased ready to use, and though sometimes stiff, readily become plastic and responsive with normal handling or the application of slight heat. Because oil-base clays are nonhardening, they do not require special care, nor do they shrink or crack. Except for inferior grades, they are very expensive, and have the disadvantageous property of being a little staining, so that it may be necessary to use a solvent to remove the oil from the tools and hands. Oil-base clays cannot be used for ceramic sculpture.

Masses of clay are wadded, squeezed, pounded, and molded until the effect required is achieved. If the sculpture is a bulky one and no armature is required, large pieces of clay can be joined by pounding them together with a block of wood or a clay mallet. If water-base clay sticks to tools, it is too wet and should be left to stiffen. If the clay is too hard, it can be sprayed lightly with water over a period of time until it becomes plastic enough to model. The manner of forming the sculpture depends somewhat on the design being created. A thin, fragile sculpture will collapse under the impact of a block or mallet, so modeling tools or fingers may have to be used; fingers or small tools will have little effect on a massive, bulky gob of clay, so large blocks of wood should be used to drive the clay into shape. The sculptor must avoid over-use of tools, especially small wood clay tools, as these may cause a tendency toward pickiness of detail and overworking of surfaces, while at the same time the basic sculptural form is neglected. In any event, the tool utilized should reflect the medium chosen and should be suitable to the overall design.

Neither water-base nor oil-base clays are suitable for permanent sculpture, because they are too easily damaged; such sculptures are therefore often converted to a permanent material. Both types of clay can be cast in permanent media (a substitution process), such as plaster or bronze, but only water-base clay can be fired into a ceramic material. Clay which is to be fired must have special handling. It must be clean, especially free of plaster which will cause spalling (large pits) and possibly cracks (Figure 94). It must also be wedged in order to free it of air pockets which would allow for the entrapment of steam during the firing process and possibly cause the sculpture to explode.

Wedging serves two purposes: it not only breaks down and eliminates air pockets, but it also distributes the moisture evenly through the mass of clay. Probably the easiest way to wedge is to cut a ball or mass of clay in half on a taut wire (Figure 95), and slam one-half of the ball down on top of the other half, which has been thrown onto a solid surface, such as a marble slab, or a heavy table covered with canvas (Figure 96). This action is repeated until, when cut on the wire, the clay mass appears to be free of trapped air pockets (Figure 97).

Figure 95.

Figure 96.

Figure 97.

Figure 94. Damage resulting from limestone and plaster in a ceramic clay body.

Crushed brick or prefired clay crumbs, known as grog, are often added to the clay in percentages up to 50% to prevent cracking of the clay body from contraction during drying or firing, and to add interesting texture and color to the clay body. Too much grog will cause the body to lose strength. It may be necessary to experiment with each clay body in order to create a satisfactory recipe. Grogs are frequently added during the wedging process, although they can also be blunged into the clay mass during its preparation.

Although common earthenware clays may appear blue, yellow, gray, tan, or red in their natural state, most fire to a red color due to their high iron content. The fired color of a clay body can be varied either by changing the firing time and temperature or by the addition of colorants, usually metallic oxides. Iron oxides produce reds, uranium oxides produce yellow, chrome oxides produce green, cobalt produces blue, copper produces black, and manganese dioxide produces tan through black. Usually, if the fired color of the clay body is white or tan, 4%-5% (by weight) of an oxide will prove effective in obtaining strong color; if the basic clay fires red, a much higher percentage of the coloring oxide will be required. Excessive use of a strong coloring oxide, such as cobalt oxide, may cause undesirable textural or color effects.

Often a clay will contain soluble substances which form a powdery white scum on fired ware, destroying their color to some extent. This scum can be eliminated by the addition of 1%-2% barium carbonate (by weight) to the clay body while blunging.

Clay sculpture which is to be preserved by firing must also have special handling. After the clay becomes leather hard (stiff enough to be handled, but soft enough to be marked or carved easily), all rigid material used as an armature must be removed and the object hollowed out, so that the walls of the sculpture are an even thickness — from 1/2" to 1½" thick, depending on the overall size of the sculpture. Uneven walls may cause cracking. If the object cannot be hollowed from the bottom, it may be necessary to cut the model into sections with a saw (a-sciotté) made of twisted strands of 24-gauge wire. The inside clay is then carved out, and the shell is put together again — after the edges are scored and coated with a thin layer of slip. Slip is a thin paste of water and clay from which the sculpture is made.

It is important that the sculpture be thoroughly dry before firing is attempted. Drying should occur slowly and may take many weeks in the case of large pieces. Rapid, uneven drying will cause uneven contraction of the clay and result in cracking. It may be

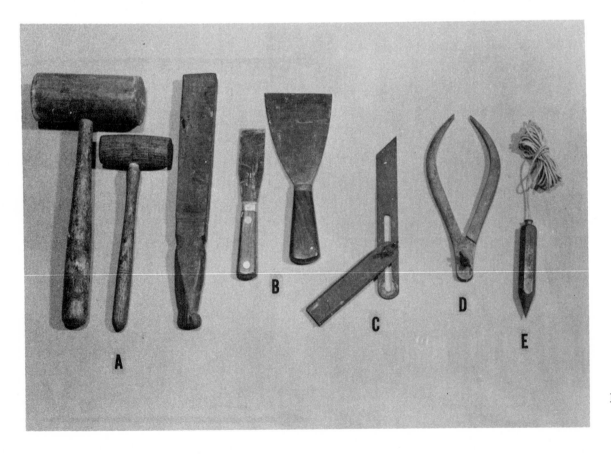

Figure 98

necessary to protect the sculpture from air currents with a cloth cover. The dried object, called "greenware," should be smoked (gently heated to drive off water remaining in the clay), to prevent the formation of steam in the clay during firing, which could result in the destruction of the object. Usually earthenware sculpture is fired to Cone 06 (about 1840° F., at a temperature rise of 68° F. per hour), but the temperature can be varied in order to attain a desired color, or degree of porosity or hardness. If additional color or textural variation is desired, the fired object, known as "bisque ware" or "bisquet," can be coated with a glaze and fired a second time. It is imperative that the glaze and the clay body be compatible at the temperature range at which the sculpture is to be fired, or the glaze may flake off (shiver) or crack (craze). If the glaze and clay body are highly incompatible, the body may crack during the cooling process because of the great difference between the rates of contraction of the glaze and the body.

Tools Required

a. Clay mallets and pounding stick of lignum vitae (Figure 98A)
b. Spatulas (Figure 98B)
c. "T" bevel or square (Figure 98C)
d. Dividers (Figure 98D)
e. Plumb bob (Figure 98E)
f. Assorted large clay modeling tools of lignum vitae (Figure 99A)
g. Medium-sized wood modeling tools (Figure 99B)
h. Plastic modeling tools (Figure 99C)
i. Modeling tools for details and a needle (Figure 99D)
j. A-sciotté (Figure 99E)

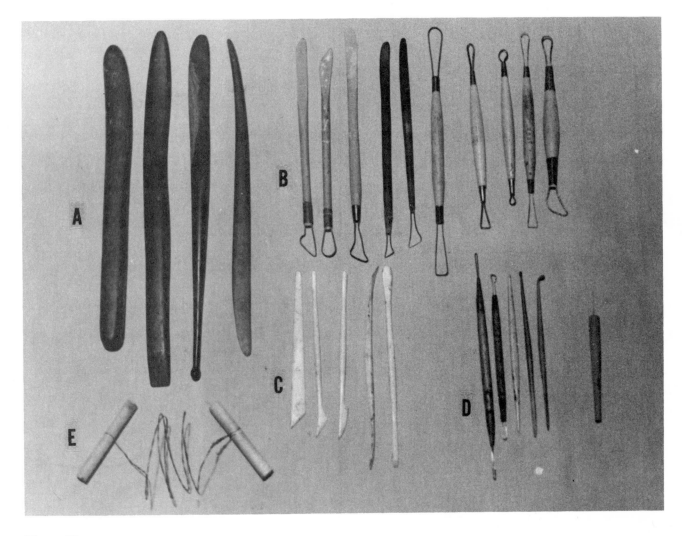

Figure 99.

Modeling in Clay

1. Prepare the clay if necessary. Water-base clay may need to be sifted, slaked, blunged, dried, and wedged before it can be used (pages 36-38).
2. Prepare the armature if one is needed (Figure 100).
3. Apply the mass of clay to the armature in small pieces (Figure 101), or pound small lumps of clay together to the rough form desired (Figures 102 and 103).
4. Shape the clay with a mallet, modeling tools, or the hands by striking, pressing, pushing, or squeezing (Figures 104, 105, 106, and 107).
5. Water may be sprayed onto the water-base clay if it tends to dry out. Between work sessions, wrap water-base clay with wet cloth and cover with sheet plastic to prevent the clay from drying out.
6. If the sculpture is to be fired, it must be hollowed and the armature removed if there is one (Figures 108, 109, 110, 111, and 112).
7. If the sculpture is to be cast, refer to the applicable substitution technique in Chapter 6.

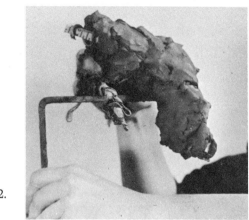

Figure 102.

Figure 103.

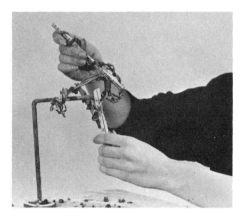

Figure 100.

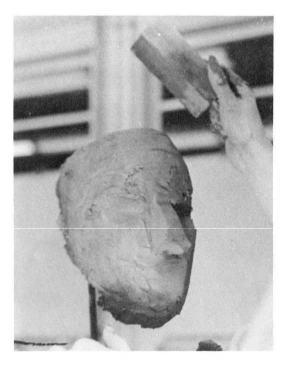

Figure 104.

Figure 101.

Figure 105.

Figure 108.

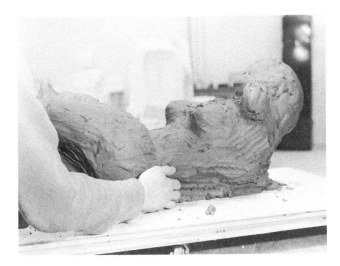

Figure 106.

Figure 109.

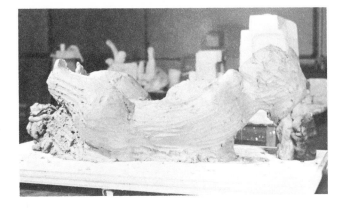

Figure 107.

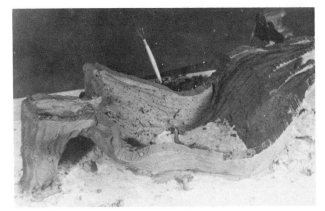

Figure 110.

Figure 111.

Figure 112.

WAX

Small wax sculpture is usually constructed in solid wax, while large wax sculpture is modeled over an armature constructed of wire or, when the wax is to be cast in metal, over a core of investment. Waxes for modeling can be obtained from commercial sources or compounded of common materials (pages 165-166). Modeling waxes usually require some adjustment of composition in order to be suitable to the season of the year or the artist. Small quantities of paraffin can be melted into the wax to stifen it for warm weather; vasoline can be used to soften the wax for winter. Waxes are usually quite transparent and cause some visual difficulty during modeling. Colorants, such as English vermilion or red or green stearate compounds, can be added to make the wax opaque, so long as they do not leave a residue

in the mold when the wax is melted out (especially if the wax is to be cast in metal).

Tools Required

a. Alcohol lamp or Bunsen burner
b. Various metal tool shapes to be heated and used to model the surface of the wax

Wax Modeling

1. A suitable wax is compounded in a double boiler.
2. The molden wax (heated just a little above its melting point) is poured onto sheets of wet formica, wet plywood, or wet paper (Figure 113). If the wax sticks, the sheets are too dry or the wax is too hot.
3. An armature is constructed and fastened to a solid base. If the wax is to be modeled over an investment core, refer to the discussion of investments on page 80.
4. Strips of warm wax formed into balls are wrapped around the armature or core, to build the necessary bulk. Wax can be melted and brushed over a core to build a uniform thickness as is required for casting purposes (Figures 114 and 115).
5. The wax can be modeled with the hands while it is warm, and it will remain pliable as long as it is being handled.
6. If necessary or desirable, metal tools, heated with an alcohol lamp or Bunsen burner, can be used to model the surface of the wax (Figures 116 and 260).
7. Textural effects can be obtained by pressing textured materials or objects into the surface of the wax.
8. Wax sculpture must be protected from concussion, abrasion, heat, and cold. Because of the great danger of loss or damage, most wax sculpture is prepared for the substitution process and cast in metal or occasionally plastic.

Figure 113.

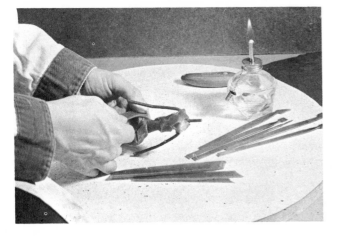

Figure 114.

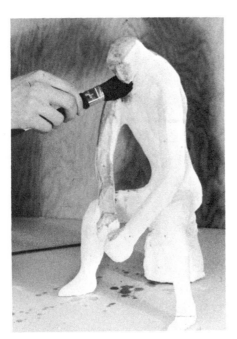

Figure 115.

Figure 116.

PLASTIC

There are two types of manipulatable plastic: plastic mass and plastic sheet. Usually plastic masses become firm only after the evaporation of a solvent or after the chemical action of a solvent or hardener. Unfortunately, because of the difficulty of controlling the hardening time and because of the toxic nature of most of the plastic masses, they have been relegated to the realm of the additive technique and are discussed in Chapter 7.

Plastic sheets, on the other hand, are primarily firm materials, and are quite resistant until they are made manageable through the application of heat or a solvent. Unlike plastic masses, the sheets are not texturally autographic — that is, the skin of the sheet is not easily altered. Rather, the entire thickness of the sheet is manipulated with pressure or torque to form a shape, a plane, or a group of planes.

Plastic sheets are fastened in rigid frames and heated, at which time, the flexible material can be stretched, pulled, molded, blown, or stamped to shape. When the plastic cools, it will retain its shape. Many plastics return to their original shape on being reheated, and may be used over again. Gloves must be worn if the plastic is to be touched by the hands during manipulation. Air pressure or vacuum can be applied to cause the sheets to expand, and molds can be used to limit the amount of expansion of the plastic or to form the desired shape, but this process is more properly a substitutive technique than a manipulative one.

Tools Required

a. A rigid frame
b. A heat lamp, hot plate, or oven
c. A pressure forming plastic press if available (Figure 117)

Modeling Plastic

1. Select or construct a rigid clamp-type frame.
2. Clamp the plastic into the frame (Figures 118, 119, and 120).
3. Heat the plastic in an oven, with heat lamps, or over a hot plate, being certain that the plastic does not sag and touch a hot surface (Figure 121).
4. Remove the heat and manipulate the plastic (Figure 122). The pressure must be maintained on the plastic until it is cool.
5. Remove the plastic from the frame and trim as required (Figure 123).
6. Formed shapes should be kept away from heat, as most of this type of plastic has a "memory" and will return to its original shape when heated.

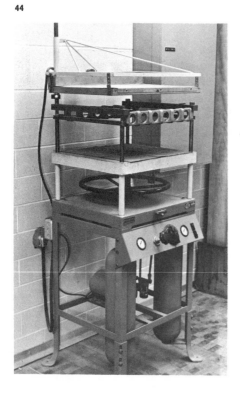

Figure 117. Di-Acro plastic press Model #18, O'Neil-Irwin Mfg. Co., Lake City, Minn.

Figure 118.

Figure 119.

Figure 120.

Figure 121.

Figure 122.

Figure 123.

METAL

Any metal which is malleable can be manipulated sculpturally. Thin sheets of the metal are hammered to shape over sandbags, anvils, stakes, or prepared wood or metal forms. Soft iron, brass, copper, silver, gold, lead, and some of their alloys are metals commonly hammered or forged by the artist. Lead, the softest metal and not as subject to hardening as other metals, is probably the simplest to form, while silver is probably the metal most often used.

The hardening that results from hammer blows on copper and silver is serious enough to cause cracking, splitting, and crumbling of the metal if it is not annealed. The annealing process differs between metals, but essentially the metal is heated to a very dull red color — in a slightly reducing flame to prevent oxidation — and allowed to cool slowly or is quenched in a liquid.

Soft irons can be shaped cold, but because of their resistance, forming is frequently accomplished while the metal is red hot from a forge. Hard coppers are also often heated for forming, but some brasses and silver tend to become very brittle at temperature ranges near cherry red. At such temperatures, the slightest blow may cause the metal to crumble.

Figure 124. *L'Avaleur*, Robert Muller, Swiss, 20th century, welded iron, Contemporary Collection of the Cleveland Museum of Art.

Tools Required

a. Forge (Figure 125)
b. Anvil with stakes (Figure 126)
c. A sand bed
d. A heating and cutting torch (Figures 383 and 384)
e. Tongs (Figure 127A)
f. Blacksmith's hammers (Figure 127C)
g. Cutting tools (Figures 128 and 384)
h. Stakes (Figure 129)

Figure 125. Johnson gas forge #133, Johnson Gas Appliance, Cedar Rapids, Iowa.

Figure 126.

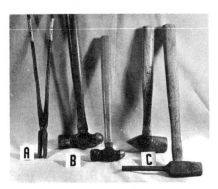

Figure 127.

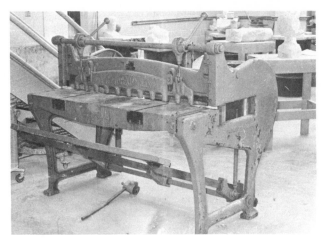

Figure 128. Pexto shear, manufactured by the Peck, Stow, and Wilcox Co.

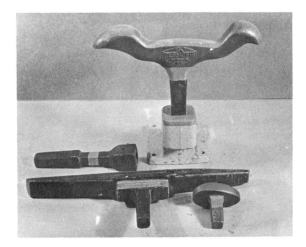

Figure 129.

Modeling Metal

1. Anneal the metal if necessary. Silver should be heated to a dull red and quenched in water or a pickle (a cleaning agent). Yellow or green gold should be heated to a cherry red, and then either quenched or allowed to cool slowly. Copper should be annealed in a muffle furnace (a reverberatory furnace) as quickly as possible; over-annealing will burn the copper yellow, causing it to become granular and extremely brittle. The easiest way to anneal copper is to heat it in iron pots while introducing steam. Steam should isolate the copper from the air until it has cooled to below 250° F.

2. Cut the sheet to the desired shape with metal saws, chisels, tin snips, a metal shear, or (except for nonferrous metals) a cutting torch.

3. Heat the metal for forming if necessary.

4. Place the metal over the appropriate sandbag, anvil, or stake, and hammer with light blows, working out from the center in a circular direction around the center (Figure 130). Blows should overlap, and the process should be repeated until the form which is desired is procured or until annealing is required (Figure 131).
5. If necessary, the metal is annealed and step 4 is repeated.

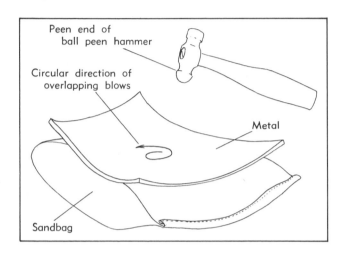

Figure 130.

Figure 131.

Repoussé

For copper or silver repoussé (a relief form which is worked from behind the face of the sculpture), the sheet should be faced with a resilient pad of pitch or wax — rather then sandbags, which will not hold the metal firmly enough.
1. Heat the sheet metal and press it onto a deep pad of warm pitch or wax (recipe on page 125).
2. Allow the metal to cool completely.
3. Use punches to depress the sheet metal into the pitch where the sculpture is to appear *raised*, working from the shallowest to the deepest area

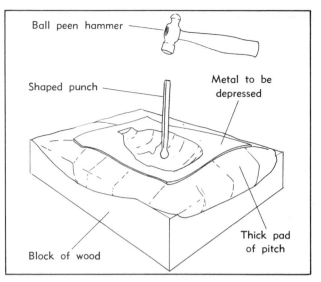

Figure 132.

(Figure 132). Remember that the relief will be seen from the face which is embedded in the pitch, so areas which are depressed with a punch will appear raised from the front.
4. Remove the repoussé for annealing if required, by warming the metal slightly and prying the metal loose from one corner.
5. Anneal and readhere the metal for additional forming.
6. The repoussé should be removed from the pitch, cleaned, and readhered, face up, on the pitch for final forming and chasing of the surface with textured punches.

OTHER MEDIA

It is of course possible to manipulate materials which are only temporarily plastic, such as some plastics, cement, plaster, and glass. Most of these materials are difficult to control because of their lack of strength, lack of adhesion, or lack of direct control of hardening time while in the plastic state. Sculptural use of these materials is therefore frequently involved in more than a single technical method.

There is also a problem, unique to glass and some plastic, that requires a concept different than that of opaque sculpture. Clear glass denies its bulk, in that it is transparent. Differing from most sculpture, the glass object does not create shadows which define its exterior shape; instead, its visual interpretation depends on refraction and reflection of light through the mass — neither defining the surface nor defining the interior of the mass itself (Figure 133). Like most other new or little-used media, glass has primarily been used in imitation of other media, involving concepts which are not suitable for transparent effects; as a result, a sculptural concept for transparent media has not yet been fully developed. Even when glass is used with color, the effects achieved are painterly, or graphic, rather than sculptural.

Figure 133. Faceted diamond.

CHAPTER 5

Subtraction

There are three approaches to the subtractive method of obtaining a three-dimensional object from a solid mass: (1) the appropriate contour or profile of the form desired is drawn on each of the faces of the material, then carved through to form a three-dimensional silhouette (Figure 135); (2) the block is worked from all directions, removing excess material until the desired form emerges (Figure 136); (3) points of the sculpture which lie on the surface of the block are located, and the block is cut back from these points until the required planes of the sculpture are revealed and subsequently join the other points (Figure 137). Each method has its advantages, depending on the form, the medium, and the artist.

Common media suitable for carving include wood, stone, cement, plaster, clay, and some plastics.

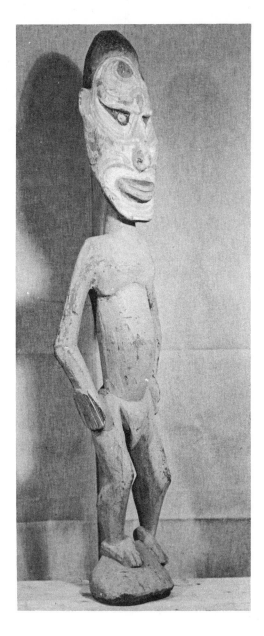

Figure 134. *Septic Ancestor Figure,* New Guinea, Bowling Green State University Collection.

49

checking (splitting). Fruit woods like apple, cherry, and pear, nut woods like walnut, hickory, and oak, and hardwoods like birch, maple, teak, rosewood, ebony, lignum vitae, snake wood, mahogany and sandlewood are all good carving woods. Pine, fir, and redwood, which tend to tear while being cut or which have uneven hardness due to the varying density of the growth rings or deposits of sap, make poor woods to carve. Because they are inexpensive, however, their use is common. Laminations of boards of the same or different kinds of wood are also frequently used (Figures 138 and 139). Varying the colors of the lamination leads to intriguing (Figure 140), but sometimes melodramatic color effects in the finished sculpture.

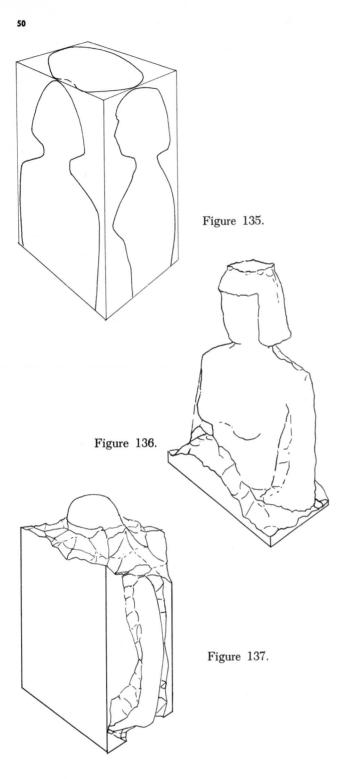

Figure 135.

Figure 136.

Figure 137.

Figure 138.

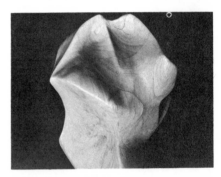

Figure 139.

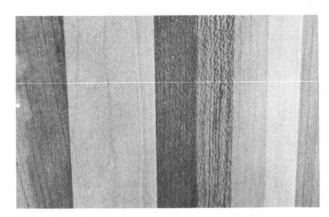

Figure 140.

WOOD

Almost any wood can be carved, but preferable woods have a few qualities in common. Choice woods cut clean, without tearing or breaking of the fibers; they are devoid of excess rosin or sap; they are hard enough to resist bruising or denting from mild blows of a blunt instrument; and they must dry without rapid deterioration or excessive

Most wood tends to check (Figure 141), as it dries. This can be minimized by removing the sap wood (the wet wood directly underneath the bark), splitting the logs through the center (or drilling the center), and painting the ends of the logs to slow the drying time. Commercially prepared wood is usually kiln dried, and checking is minimized — provided the wood is stored in a place which has an even temperature and humidity, or is coated with a heavy wax until it is used and finished. Checking

should be considered a normal action of wood and the sculptor should allow for it and make use of it. If necessary, fillers or beeswax mixed with the appropriate color oil paint can be used to pack the checks. Packing these checks may prevent the wood from chipping along the edge of the cracks encountered during carving. Frequently, in time, checks in wood will close. If a hard filler, such as plastic wood or plaster, is used in the cracks, the wood may be forced to split in other places when the original checks swell closed.

All wood has grain, although some grain is not obvious. The grain of the wood should be respected: cuts tangent to growth rings result in broad grain (Figure 142); cuts at right angles to growth rings give narrow grain (Figure 140); cuts against the grain cause the tool to dive or dig into the wood. Only cuts across the grain or with the grain permit the sculptor to maintain control over the medium.

Tools Required

a. Sharpening stone (Figure 143A)
b. Mallet, preferably of lignum vitae wood (Figure 143B)
c. Gouges, (Figures 143C, 143D, and 143E)
d. Flat chisels (Figure 143F)
e. Skew chisel (Figure 143G)
f. Parting or "V" chisel (Figure 143H)
g. Sharpening slips (Figure 143I)
h. Bent chisel (Figure 143J)
i. Spoon chisel (Figure 143K)
j. Bench lag bolt (Figure 143L)
k. An assortment of rifflers and rasps (Figure 143M)

Figure 141.

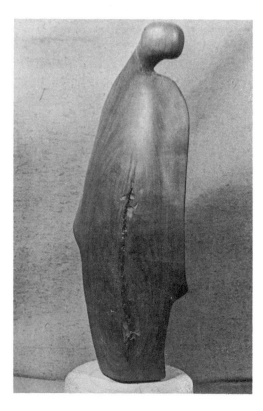

Figure 142. *Flapper,* walnut.

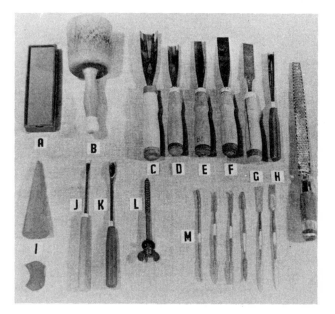

Figure 143.

52

SUBTRACTION

Additional tools for carving wood include air hammer (with an assortment of suitable chisels), bucksaw (Figure 144B), handsaw (Figure 144A), coping saw (Figure 144C), band saw, electric power tools such as grinders and sanders, a gasoline powered chain saw, and a sledge hammer and steel wedges for splitting away bark or large masses of wood.

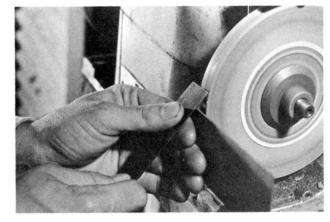

Figure 146.

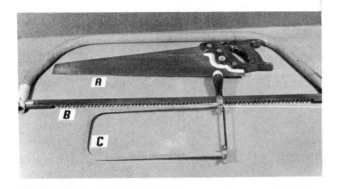

Figure 144.

pushed forward (Figure 147). The burr is removed by repeating the action on the fine side of the combination stone. Pulling the tool backward over a leather block will hone the tool to a fine edge. Metal tools should be lightly oiled when not in use.

Wood Carving

1. Fill the checks with beeswax.
2. Remove large unwanted areas of wood by sawing or cutting with a gouge (Figures 148 and 149).

Tool Care

Most newly purchased wood chisels require only honing for use, though some also require sharpening, as the tools have only been shaped, and some, like tool blanks, even require shaping. Wood chisels should be made from high-grade steel that is heat tempered so the tool will hold an edge. The tool is first ground to shape on a wheel, by holding the tool at a right angle to the wheel (Figure 145). Hollow grind the blade next, using the circumference of the wheel to bevel the tool (Figure 146). Care must be exercised while grinding the tool to prevent overheating and burning the tool. The tool is now finished on the coarse side of a combination stone, which is saturated with oil. The bevel is held against the stone and

Figure 147.

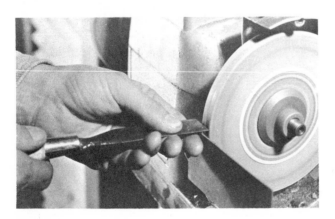

Figure 145.

Figure 148.

Figure 149.

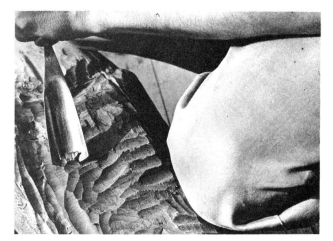

Figure 151.

Figure 152.

3. Lock the wood to a bench in a wood vise, with a large bench screw or with clamps and a bench stop (Figure 150). If none of these is satisfactory, the wood can be placed on bags of sand or in a barrel filled with sand.

4. Gouges are used to rough out the shape. The tools are pushed by hand or struck with a wood mallet (Figure 151). In order to prevent fatigue, air hammers with special chisels can be used. Start the tool into the wood at a 45° angle, but don't take too big a bite, and don't cut against the grain, as

Figure 150.

this may cause the tool to dive into the wood and jam. If the tool jams, do not strike the side of the tool or pry up on the handle or blade; instead, lift the wood by holding the chisel blade in such a way that the wood hangs down, then strike down on the wood to drive the wood off of the chisel. Do not lever with the tool, as this will probably break the edge, if not the whole end, of the tool. Remove long strips of wood rather than chunks (Figure 152).

5. Use small gouges to clarify the form and simplify the emerging shapes. Change gouges to suit the area being carved.

6. Use flat chisels to clean up textures left by gouges, if desirable, and to sharpen contours or edges (Figures 153 and 154).

7. Rasp and sand areas which are to be free of tool marks (Figure 155).

Figure 153.

Figure 154.

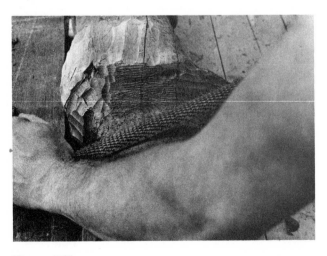

Figure 155.

Finishing

Some woods such as rosewood, teak, and ebony have natural oils or waxes and do not need an artificial sealer or finish, other than polishing with a soft cloth. Other woods, however, require a protective coat, which prevents moisture intake, the collection of dirt, and perhaps enhances the natural color of the grain. Probably the simplest and best finish for wood is two or three brushed and rubbed layers of boiled linseed oil. The only difficulty with linseed oil is that it tends to darken light wood. Transparent paste wax such as floor wax or shoe polish can be used as directed for the product, and serves satisfactorily, though they may cause too much shine for some sculpture. Lacquer can be sprayed on and rubbed with steel wool to give a nonglossy surface. The wood can also be treated with commercial stain, bleach, household paint, oil paint, acrylic polymer paint, and even gesso. Unwanted paint can be removed by mixing a paste of wallpaper paste and lye, which is painted on and then cleaned off with water or turpentine after the paint has become sufficiently soft. Use *caution* with this solution, as contact with the paste can result in severe burns.

Figure 156. *Horse*, carved soapstone, China.

STONE

Rock can be divided into three classifications: sedimentary rock (sandstone and limestone), metamorphic rock (marble, serpentine, steatite or soapstone, and slate), and igneous rock (granite, gabbros, and basalts). Sedimentary rock is stone formed from layers of sand, gravel, and shell deposits, which have been under pressure, and have become cemented together. Metamorphic rock is sedimentary rock that has been subjected to great heat and pressure until it has fused. Igneous rock is a solidified mass which at one time was fluid, perhaps through the heat of volcanic action. It is the hardest of the three classifications of rock to carve, but it is among the most durable, and takes an excellent polish. In most cases, the favored rock of the sculptor is metamorphic rock, usually marble — which, like limestone of the sedimentary class is fairly easy to carve, but the durability of which is questionable. Softer metamorphic rock — like some steatite — can be carved with a penknife and scratched with a fingernail. These rocks are not at all durable and frequently have a greasy or soapy feeling, from which they get their common name, soapstone. Sedimentary rocks are often visibly layered or stratified. These stratifications are known as bedding planes. When carving stratified rocks, it is advantageous to keep the bedding planes in their natural positions; otherwise, when utilized out-of-doors, the stone may weather rapidly and decay. Igneous and metamorphic rock and many limestones, which do not have these stratifications, and, therefore, do not have natural bedding planes, are known as "freestones."

Tools Required

a. Carvers hammers (Figures 157A and 157B)

b. A large point (Figure 157C)

c. Pitching tool or "bullset" (Figure 157D)

d. A tool blank to be forged to special shapes (Figure 157E)

e. Machine tooth chisel (Figure 157F)

f. Universal bush hammer (Figure 157G)

g. Combination pick and bush hammer (Figure 157H)

h. Small point (Figures 157I and 157J)

i. Flat chisel, fine (Figure 157K)

j. Flat chisel, broad (Figure 157L)

k. Roundel or gouge (Figure 157M)

l. Flat-toothed chisel (Figure 157N)

m. Toothed chisels (Figures 157O, 157P, and 157Q)

n. Nine-point bush chisel (Figure 157R)

o. Square bush hammer (Figure 157S)

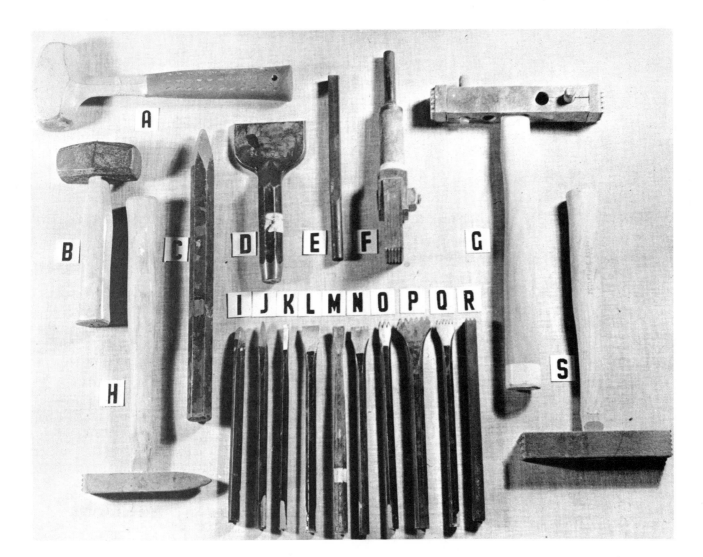

Figure 157.

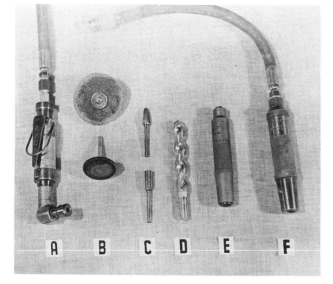

Figure 158.

Power Tools
a. Pneumatic grinder (Figure 158A)
b. Grinding wheels (Figure 158B)
c. Grinding burrs (Figure 158C)
d. Carbide-tipped drill (to be used in an electric drill) (Figure 158D)
e. One-half inch straight line pneumatic hammer (Figure 158E)
f. Three-quarter inch straight line pneumatic hammer, with attached hose and snap-on fitting (Figure 158F)
g. Tool blank (Figure 159A)
h. Point (Figure 159B)
i. Machine chisel (Figure 159C)
j. Cleanup chisel (Figure 159D)
k. Marble tooth chisel (Figures 159E and 160E)
l. Ripper (Figure 159F)
m. Frosting chisel, large point (Figures 159G and 160D)

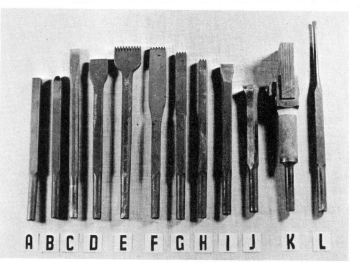

Figure 159.

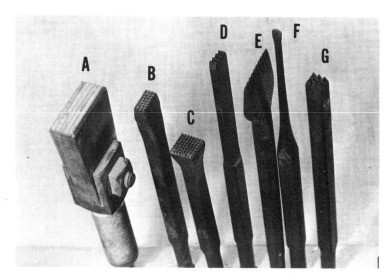

Figure 160.

n. Nine-point chisel (Figures 159H and 160G)
o. Frosting tool, small point (Figures 159I and 160B)
p. Frosting tool, fine point (Figures 159J and 160C)
q. Machine bush chisel (Figures 159K and 160A)
r. Carvers or plug drill (Figures 159L and 160F)

Other Tools

Carborundum slips, Wet or Dry sandpaper, stone wedges, feathers, plugs, grub saw (a two-man saw which uses sand or shot instead of teeth), rifflers, rasps, and a sledge hammer.

Stone tools are usually purchased preshaped, tempered, and sharpened, but on occasion must be forged by the sculptor. The end of the tool blank is placed in the red coals (mixed coke and charcoal) of a forge until the tool is cherry red, at which time it is hammered to shape. The tool is then replaced in the fire; when the tip is cherry red (1650°-1700° F.), it is removed from the fire and dipped one-half inch into a cold brine solution of 2 oz. rock salt to 11 gallons of water, for six seconds. The tool is then quickly rubbed on fine sandpaper in order to reveal the temper. If the temper is correct for granite, the tip colors will be white, to gold, to bronze, to purple, to blue. This banding should extend only three-quarters of an inch from the tip of the tool. When the tool has cooled to this temper, it is quickly dipped into the brine to hold the temper. Marble tools should be hardened to a bluish purple and quenched in cold water rather than brine.

Stone Carving

1. Determine the bedding of the stone. If the bottom is not flat, it must be carved flat.
2. Split away excess stone with plugs and feathers. The line of the split is marked, and pilot holes are drilled with a carvers or plug drill. Larger

Figure 162.

holes following the pilot holes are then drilled with a carbide drill. Feathers are inserted in the holes with the divisions between the feathers parallel to the line of the split; feathers are then lightly greased, and wedged into place with the plugs. The plugs are then struck lightly in order. The impact against the plugs is increased until the sound of the stone goes "dead" and the stone splits.

The stone can also be split by drilling a series of holes along the break line (Figure 161), then chiseling between the holes to open the stone (Figure 162). It may be necessary to pound tapered wedges into the holes to help put a strain on the block along the break line.

3. The pitcher is then used to remove the remaining large amounts of excess stone, by placing it at right angles to the surface and parallel to the edge of the stone, about 1″ back from the edge. The pitcher — or bullset, as it is sometimes called — is then struck with a heavy hammer, causing large spalls to break off (Figure 163). The pitcher should be struck repeatedly as it is moved side-

Figure 161.

Figure 163.

ways back and forth along a line parallel to the edge. Pitchers can be used as long as there are flat areas on the stone. If the surface is too coarse to utilize the pitcher, a groove, known as a "chase," about 1″ wide should be carved along the edge of the stone with a point, in order to give the pitcher some place to grip (Figure 164).

4. A heavy point is used to rough out the basic form. This tool is held at a 40°–60° angle to the surface of the stone, depending on the hardness of the material. It is then struck repeatedly, until a piece of stone spalls off (Figures 165 and 166). If the tool dives and sticks, the angle is too

steep, and the point will break off. If the angle is too shallow, the tool will not chip; it will slip instead. Most carving of the sculpture, with either hand or power tools, should be done with the point.

5. The form is refined with the light point, used in the same manner as the heavy point.

6. Further leveling and texturing is managed with the tooth chisel (claw tool) (Figure 167). The claw or tooth chisel will not spall off large pieces of stone — it tends, rather, to grind and powder the surface — but it does leave furrow-like lines (Figure 168).

Figure 164.

Figure 167.

Figure 165.

Figure 166.

Figure 168.

7. Use frosting tools to smooth away these furrows, flattening the surface wherever desired (Figure 169).

8. Where a smooth surface and sharp angles or edges are required, as in Figure 170, flat chisels are used. Flat chisels, though handled in the same way as tooth chisels, will not leave furrows, and they prepare the surface for polishing (Figure 171).

9. Rough surfaces of soft rock, like marble and limestone can be cut and smoothed at this time by rasps and rifflers (Figure 172). These tools are not hard enough to be used on igneous rocks.

Figure 171.

Figure 169.

Figure 172.

Figure 170.

10. The stone is finished and polished by rubbing with succeedingly finer grades of Wet or Dry sandpaper, and then washed and rubbed with cloth. It is then rubbed with putty powder paste, and finally washed and rubbed with a cloth. A thorough finishing sequence follows:

a. rub with fine emery stone; wash and rub with cloth;

b. rub with course sandstone; wash and rub with cloth;

c. rub with fine sandstone; wash and rub with cloth;

d. rub with pumice stone; wash and rub with cloth;

e. rub with an English hone; wash and rub with cloth;

f. rub with putty powder and powdered oxalic acid on a damp rag; wash and rub with cloth.

CEMENT AND PLASTER

Portland cement ranges from dark gray to white in color, and it hardens when mixed with water. These cements acquire strength with age, and require water in order to complete the tempering cycle. For this reason, cement sculpture should be kept damp, if not wet, for 28 days from the time that the cement is poured, at which time the cement will have reached its greatest strength. Cements which are mixed only with water are known as neat cements; those mixed with fine filler, such as sand, are known as mortars; and those mixed with various-sized fillers, like sand and gravel, are known as concrete. Chemically stable materials, such as marble chips, brick dust, iron filings, perlite, zonalite, terrazo chips, ground glass, pebbles, sawdust, and so on, can be added to cement in amounts up to 50% by volume to vary weight and create interesting textures and colors. The dry ingredients should be thoroughly mixed, then cool water folded in, to make a paste with the consistency of thick mud. Additional water or cement can be added to adjust the thickness of the matrix as required. The common problem of surface cracking (Figure 173) can to a great extent be eliminated by mixing an extremely thick mixture and tamping rather then pouring the matrix into a container. Special pigments (mortar colors) can be added to the aggregate to color the cement. Manufacturers' directions must be carefully followed, as misuse of the pigments can destroy the binding qualities of the cement.

Number 1 white casting plaster and number 1 white molding plaster are the plasters preferred for casting or carving, or for use as a binder for plaster-based, carvable aggregates. Other plasters are available, but most tend to be too soft, grayish, or have too little adhesion to be desirable. Plasters, like cement, can be mixed with aggregate materials, but frequently

Figure 174.

Figure 175.

Figure 176.

Figure 177.

Figure 178.

Figure 173.

these aggregates will draw water from the plaster, causing the plaster to become extremely hard, gray, and glossy. Plaster should be mixed by slowly sifting the powder through the fingers into a pan of still cool water (Figures 174, 175, and 176) until the plaster rises slightly above the water level (Figure 177). If the plaster is dumped into the water too rapidly, an island will be formed, preventing the water from being absorbed by the plaster. The resulting mixture will be too thin, yielding a soft, porous, slow-hardening plaster. If too much plaster is added to the water, the result will be a rapid-setting, lumpy, dense, hard plaster. After all of the plaster has picked up water in the mixing bowl, the mixture is mixed into a slurry (Figure 178). At this point the hardening action is accelerated. Neither water nor plaster should be added to the matrix after mixing has started. Aggregates which are damp can be added at this time, but, if possible, aggregate materials should be mixed with the dry plaster. Plaster aggregates usually harden rapidly, in some cases in less than 4 minutes after mixing is started. Normal plaster will harden in 15-20 minutes. Most of the strength of the plaster is established by the time the plaster becomes warm (heat of crystallization), but a little additional strength is gained during the following 24 hours. Many of the same aggregate materials used in cement can be used in plaster, and in increased amounts, if desired. Tests should be made to check for setting time and hardness. Some aggregates may destroy the setting ability of the plaster; others, such as a mixture of ground glass and iron filings, may slow the setting time slightly and make the aggregate too hard to be worked with ordinary tools. Specially compounded dry pigments, usually in amounts of less than 10%, can be added to the water to color the plaster. Ordinary tempera paint and large amounts of dry tempera pigment are not satisfactory, because in certain cases they destroy the hardness of the plaster or because the plaster may bleach away the color.

Plaster and Cement Carving

1. Dry mix the ingredients, then mix the matrix.
2. Pour or tamp the fluid matrix into a waterproof container such as a plastic-lined cardboard box or a shellacked wooden box (Figure 179). Shake or tamp the matrix while the box is being filled in order to release air bubbles.
3. When the matrix stiffens enough to be handled without damage (2-8 hours for cement, 10-20 minutes for plaster), remove the box (Figure 180) and carve the rough form with any suitable tool such as a spoon, knife, hacksaw blade, pick, chisel, or

Figure 179.

Figure 180.

wood tool. Rasps, saws, and similar tools which will become clogged by the muggy medium should be avoided.

4. Permit the roughed form to harden and dry to a point where it can be worked with rasps, files, and eventually sandpaper. Cement requires 3-10 days to reach this state, but care must be taken to keep it from drying too rapidly, or it will lose its strength and crack or crumble. Special tools are available to work wet plaster, but it will usually take a week or more for plaster to dry enough to be rasped with an ordinary rasp. Do not force cement or plaster to dry with heat, as cracking may result.

Finishing

Cements have greater resistance to weather than plasters, but if either is to be utilized out-of-doors, some protective coating must be applied to the sculpture to prevent the porous bodies from absorbing dirt, and to prevent intake of water, which will destroy plaster and can rot cement. In freezing temperatures, absorbed water will freeze, expand, and fracture plaster and cement or, at the least, cause spalling. Recipes for finishing plaster and cement are given on pages 127-128.

CLAY

Clay which is to be carved is prepared in the same manner as clay which is to be modeled (pages 36 to 38). It is preferable, though, that clay which is to be carved be of a little stiffer consistency than modeled clay. Wire and wood tools are used to expose form and to complete detail instead of the pounding block or the hands. Some care must be taken that the clay carving does not become a study of detail rather than a sculptural unit. Normally this danger is avoided by combining the manipulative technique with the subtractive technique when dealing with clay.

Tools Required

a. Clay mallet (Figure 181A)
b. Wire modeling tools (Figure 181B)
c. Wood modeling tools (Figure 181C)
d. A spatula (Figure 181D)
e. A-sciotté, a saw made of twisted strands of wire (Figure 181E)

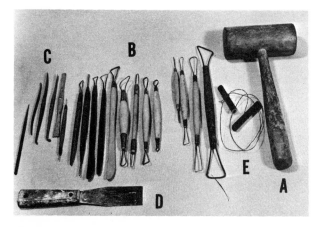

Figure 181.

Tool Care

All tools should be cleaned and dried after use. Iron or steel tools should be rubbed with an oily cloth before storage.

Clay Carving

1. Wedge ceramic clay to eliminate air bubbles (Figures 95, 96, and 97).
2. Pound the clay into a large mass with the mallet (Figure 182). If the clay sculpture will require an

armature (pages 31-35), the clay should be pounded around this support.
3. Allow the clay to stiffen if necessary.
4. Cut away excess clay with the a-sciotté by drawing the wire back and forth across and through the clay (Figure 183).
5. Refine the form with the wire tools. Use as large a tool as possible at all times (Figures 184, 185, and 186).
6. Scrapers and stamps may be used to create texture (Figure 187). The scrapers are drawn across the surface in order to leave marks, not to remove marks (Figure 188). Do not utilize the scraper to smooth or slick surfaces. Stamps are objects with textures on their surfaces that can be transferred to the clay by pressing the object against the clay (Figure 189). Tools, wire screen, bolts, screws, coins, and so on can be used as stamps.
7. Hollow and allow the sculpture to dry slowly, out of drafts (Figure 190). It may be necessary to cover the sculpture with a box of some kind to slow the drying time. It is important that the walls of the sculpture be of consistent thickness (between one-half of an inch and one inch), or the walls may crack during the firing process (Figure 190).

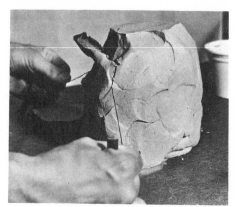

Figure 182.

Figure 183.

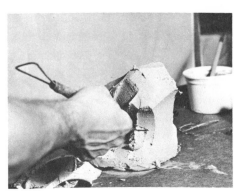

Figure 184.

Figure 187.

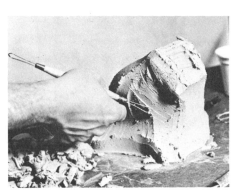

Figure 185.

Figure 188.

Figure 186.

Figure 189.

8. If the sculpture is to be cast in plaster, it should be prepared for casting as indicated in Chapter 6, and not hollowed.

9. If it is necessary to preserve the sculpture in its plastic state for any length of time, a wet cloth should be draped over the clay, and it should then be covered with sheet plastic.

Figure 190.

PLASTIC

Among those plastic materials that are available for carving, the most suitable are some of the acrylics, the phenolics, the polyesters, and the epoxies. Although frequently used in their "neat" state, filler materials are often added to the plastic to form aggregates. These fillers substantially decrease the cost of the medium, as well as add bulk, strength, resistance to warping and shrinkage, and color; they also cause opacity. Aggregate plastics purchased from commercial sources are usually more "pure" than studio-made aggregates, and are a great deal more expensive.

If the block is to be prepared from liquid state by the sculptor, care should be exercised in selection of the plastic, and the manufacturer's directions should be followed to-the-letter. Only certain polyesters and epoxies can be cast easily into blocks over 3″ thick without serious warping, shrinking, and cracking problems. For large masses of plastic, the commercial resins sold for use with glass fibers will give the fewest problems. It may even be necessary to build large masses by pouring the plastic in layers. Acrylics are highly susceptible to these faults; therefore, this type of plastic mass should be obtained from commercial sources if possible.

Acrylics, polyesters, and epoxies are fairly easy to work with ordinary tools. Objects can be rough-shaped by sawing with wood or metal saws. A straight saw having 8-10 teeth per inch, with very little set, is best suited to this work. The saw should be held straight, without twist, or the plastic may crack. These plastics can be drilled to remove material by using a heated wire, or with an ordinary twist drill for metal — but which has been reground for drilling brass. The cutting edge of the drill should be ground flat instead of angled, in order to produce a scraping edge instead of a cutting edge. A slow-turning drill is preferred, but high-speed drills can be used if the hole is lubricated with water or kerosene to prevent burning of the plastic. Never drill cold plastic. The material should always be warmed to at least 70° F. before drilling is attempted. Probably most of the final cutting of the plastic will be done with files. Flats, half-rounds, and rat-tail files will be most useful, so long as they have not been dulled or gummed from filing on metal or other materials. Files should be cleaned frequently with a wire brush. Scrapers can be used to remove material or to texture the surface of the plastic. Scrapers should be held at a 45° angle to the work and pulled toward the operator. Hacksaw blades, old files, knives, or tool steel blanks can be ground to shapes or textures desired. The wire burr

which is left from shaping and sharpening the scraper blade should be removed before use. Shaping tools and grinding wheels that can be used in the chuck or collet of an electric drill or flexible shaft can be used to cut in tight spots. Sanding disks can also be used in these chucks to cut away or smooth larger areas.

Common phenolics are more difficult to work than acrylics, polyesters, or epoxies. Probably the only really useful carving tools for most phenolics are sanding disks, grinding tools, or carbide bits in flexible shafts. Phenolics should be cast in their approximate shape and size, and finished with a minimum of grinding. They can be polished with #400 waterproof sandpaper.

Polystyrene, which has been foamed (styrofoam) can be easily carved with the simplest of devices, knives, files, sandpaper, hot soldering irons, hot wire, or even heated metal tools. Because of the extreme softness of this plastic, it is usually carved for armatures (page 34) or to be cast in metal (page 92).

Tools Required

a. Wood saws (Figure 191A)
b. Hacksaws (Figure 191B)
c. Coping saw (Figure 191C)
d. Files (Figure 191D)
e. Flexible shaft (Figure 191E)
f. Electric drill (Figure 191F)
g. Drills (twist) (Figure 191G)
h. Scrapers (Figure 191H)
i. Electric soldering iron (Figure 191I)
j. Sanding disks (Figure 192A)
k. Wire brush (Figure 192B)
l. Wire wheel (Figure 192C)
m. Buffing wheels and compounds (Figure 192D)
n. Hot wire (Figure 192E)

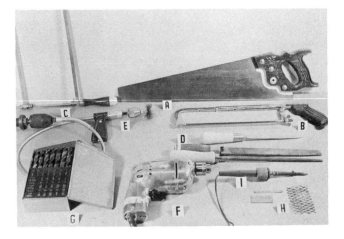

Figure 191.

Figure 192.

Carving Plastic

1. Pour and cure the block (pages 64 and 121), if the plastic is not procured in solid form.
2. Draw the design on the appropriate faces of the block with a grease pencil or scratch it in with a metal scribe.
3. Saw excess material away.
4. Use files, sanders, shaping tools, and grinders to complete the shaping of the sculpture.
5. If desired, the sculpture can be sanded or textured by scraping the surface with a scraper, by impressing hot stamps into the plastic, or by brushing with a wire wheel.
6. Foamed polystyrene-type materials cannot be polished, but acrylic plastics can be polished in accordance with the directions on page 121, and polyesters, epoxies, and phenolics can be polished by sanding with #400 Wet or Dry sandpaper.

OTHER MEDIA

Bone and ivory are other materials which can be utilized for the subtractive technique, but are not extensively used in our culture because of some natural limitations (Figure 193). Both bone and ivory are easily obtained, though limited in size, and are readily shaped through the use of hand or power tools, incorporating cutting, grinding, or shaping bits. Both materials tend to yellow, warp, and check with age. Even though these media are easily carved, they still have considerable strength; as a result, highly intricate and delicate carving can be achieved.

Figure 193. *Madonna and Child*, ivory triptych, French, 14th century, The Cleveland Museum of Art, Purchase from the J. H. Wade Fund.

CHAPTER 6

Substitution

Substitution is the process of casting in one medium what has been formed in another medium. The technique has traditionally been an imitative device, in which copies of a model have been the goal of the foundryman. The contemporary artist has been utilizing the technique as a method of creating a shell from which the sculpture is created. The casting is treated as the beginning of the sculpture, not as the final goal of the artist.

There are four kinds of molds normally used in casting processes: waste molds, piece molds, flexible molds, and sand molds. The waste mold is a unique mold; it produces only one cast and is eventually destroyed in order to remove the cast. It is the most accurate mold type for the student, but frequently causes trouble during the process of removing the mold from the cast. The piece mold is similar to the waste mold except that it is usually divided into a greater number of sections; as a result, the mold can be removed from the cast in pieces in such a way as to save the mold for reuse. Piece molds are subject to

Figure 194. *Altar to Another God,* cast aluminum.

some surface blemishes and distortion, due to shrinkage and warping of the mold sections and because of the flashing marks left by the seams between the mold sections (Figure 195). Some distortion also stems from the fact that piece molds can seldom be reassembled in exactly the same position. Regardless of these disadvantages, piece molds are probably the best for all-around use.

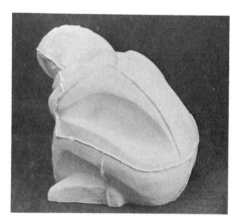

Figure 195.

Flexible molds may be molds which are elastic enough that they can be removed from fairly complex master (model) shapes without damage to the mold or the model. Flexible molds are subject to excess distortion and shrinkage, and have other disadvantages due to their chemical make-up. Sand molds are, in a sense, waste molds, because they are used only once, but they are similar to piece molds in the way in which they are assembled. Because of the nature of the sand, these molds are limited in complexity and, for all practical purposes, limited as to the casting medium.

Molds are constructed of many materials. Waste molds are usually constructed of plaster-based mixtures, sulphur, sometimes hard waxes and occasionally resins. Piece molds are constructed of plaster, cement, metal, wood, waxes, fiberglass, and others. Flexible molds are made from natural rubber, glue (gelatin), and plastics. Sand molds are formed from mixtures of earth materials, including various grades of sand, loam, and clay, and sometimes artificial binders.

Models for plaster molds are usually made in modeling clay; occasionally models of plaster, plastics, metal, and wood are used. Models used in sand molds are formed from any hard dry material; wood, plaster, or metal are used most commonly. If the cast is to be in molten metal over 1500° F., volatile materials — which pass off in small volumes of gas and little ash — may be used as models or parts of

models by simply imbedding these materials in investments or in sand, and then either burning out the model before pouring the metal, or pouring the molten metal directly onto the model in such a way that the heat of the metal burns away the model.

The kind of mold which should be constructed for a casting depends on the nature of the model, the accuracy required of the cast, the number of casts required, and the media to be used for the cast.

Waste Mold

1. Divide the model into the fewest number of divisions which will allow removal of the model without damage to the mold. Sometimes a clay model can be completely dug out of a waste mold, in which case the model need not be divided at all (Figure 196).
2. Press shim stock (brass or aluminum .008″ thick) or flexible strips of stiff plastic into the model along the division lines (Figure 197). The shims must overlap tightly, and the top edges of the shims must be trimmed evenly (Figure 198).

Figure 196.

Figure 197.

Figure 198.

3. Add plaster to water that has been tinted with bluing; a thick mixture is required (page 60).

4. Snap a thin (1/8") blue plaster warning coat onto the model by dipping the fingers into the plaster and snapping the fingers at the model with some force (Figures 199 and 200). The plaster must come into positive contact with the model in order to produce a sharp impression. Take care that no bubbles of air are trapped under the warning coat, especially in corners and crevices.

5. After the model is covered with a layer of blue plaster, scrape all of the edges — not the surfaces of the shims — clean of plaster (Figure 201).

6. A thick batch of white plaster is then mixed and snapped on the blue warning coat, in order to strengthen the blue coat. Air pockets must still be avoided at this stage. This thin coat must be strengthened by Step 8 as soon as possible to prevent the coat from cracking and falling off of the model (Figure 202).

7. Clean the edges of the shims.

8. Apply additional plaster with a spatula or similar tool to cover the entire mold to a thickness

Figure 202.

Figure 203.

Figure 204.

Figure 199.

Figure 200.

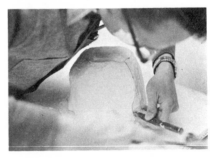

Figure 205.

Figure 201.

of about 1" or thicker, except for the shim lines which must remain exposed (Figure 203).

9. Scrape the shims clean.

10. After the plaster hardens, remove the mold by tapping along the line of shims with a thin chisel, alternately from one side of the mold to the other on the same shim line, until the mold begins to separate (Figures 203, 204, and 205).

Figure 206.

Figure 207.

Figure 208.

16. Soak the mold in water, then fill the mold and allow the cast to harden. Pour the casting as carefully as possible, in order to avoid air bubbles (Figure 210).
17. Remove the bindings from the mold.
18. Progressing from the weakest area of the casting to the strongest, usually from the top to the bottom, chisel the mold away from the cast. The layer of blue plaster next to the surface of the cast will indicate that the cast is about to be revealed and that great care must be taken that the surface of the cast is not scarred by an impatient sculptor, or that the cast is not broken by rough handling. Weak areas of the cast should be supported so that the shock of chipping does not fracture the cast (Figure 211).

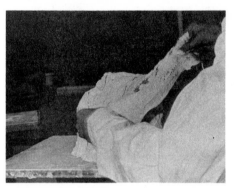

Figure 209.

Figure 210.

Figure 211.

11. When the mold opens a crack, rock the pieces of the mold gently and work the mold until it separates from the model. If additional force is required to start the mold to open, use a thick chisel along the shim line (Figures 206 and 207).
12. Remove the shims and any parts of the model which may have remained in the mold. Wash the mold clean with water and a soft brush. Overwashing will destroy detail and cause the surface of the mold to go soft.
13. Apply the proper mold separator to the mold (Figure 208).
14. Assemble the mold and bind it with wire (Figure 231), heavy rubber bands cut from inner tubes (Figure 232), metal spring clamps or burlap strips soaked in plaster (Figure 209).
15. Mix enough plaster to fill the mold. Avoid stirring bubbles into the paster.

Piece Mold

The area requiring the greatest attention in a piece mold is the undercut — a place on a model which, because of its shape, restricts removal of the mold. If for instance, a bottle shape is being cast, the mold which shapes the inside of the bottle will be too large to be taken out of the mouth of the bottle; in such a cast, the neck and lip would be called an undercut. It would be necessary to divide the mold in such a way that the mold could be removed in sections, eliminating the restricting effect of the undercut.

Piece Mold (Soft Model)

1. Divide the model into as few, and as simple, sections as possible — presenting no undercuts (Figure 196).
2. Press shim stock into the model along the dividing lines (Figure 197). Registration of the mold will be aided if the shim line of each section contains a sharp "S" curve or if a shim is folded into a "V" shape (Figure 212). Shims must lap tightly, and edges should be evenly trimmed (Figure 198).

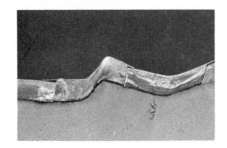

Figure 212.

3. Mix a thick plaster (page 60) and snap a layer onto the model to build up the mold. Though not necessary, a warning coat of blue plaster is often useful. Care must be exercised to avoid trapping air on the face of the model and within the first half-inch of the thickness of the mold.
4. Clean the edges of the shims.
5. Apply additional layers of plaster with a spatula or similar tool to an all-over thickness of 1″ or thicker for larger molds. If the mold consists of many sections, loops of wire may be embedded in the plaster of each section before the plaster hardens, to be used in tying the mold together again (Figure 217).
6. Clean the edges of the shims.
7. Number the sections of the mold, in order to avoid confusion during reassembly of the mold.
8. Use a thick chisel along the shim lines to loosen the mold (Figures 204 and 205). Remove the mold from the model, and wash the mold clean. Over-washing should be avoided. If difficulty is

encountered in removing sections of the mold, a blast of compressed air — between model and mold — may break the mild vacuum which forms when sections of the mold are lifted from the model.

Piece Mold (Hard Model)

1. Treat the model with a separator to prevent the plaster of the mold from clinging to the model (Figure 213). For wood or stone models, use two coats of shellac cut with alcohol, and a final coat of stearine dissolved in kerosene. For plaster models, use green soap or commercial mold soap, well lathered on the surface of the sculpture; rinse in cold water. It may be necessary to treat the model several times before a satisfactory surface is procured. For metal models, use a light coating of motor oil, 3-in-1 Oil, or a kerosene-stearine solution.
2. Mark the model into sections which will eliminate all undercuts.
3. Build a clay wall ¼″ to ½″ thick, and about 1″ high along the dividing lines to isolate one section of the mold (Figure 214). These walls should have dimples pressed into them with a marble or similar device, to aid in keying the sections for reassembly. It may be necessary to lay the model on its side, and to make the mold sections one side at a time. If the mold is made one side at a time, the lines dividing the halves should be the division lines for the retaining shells referred to in Step 8. Avoid making the isolated sections too large, or it

Figure 213.

Figure 214.

will be difficult to fill the section with plaster (Figure 215).

4. Warm stearine-kerosene solution or oil is then painted in the isolated area if required.

5. Pour plaster inside of the clay walls and vibrate or puddle the plaster with a stick to release trapped air (Figure 216). A sharp rap on the stand supporting the mold may release bubbles from the surface of the model.

6. Embed a wire loop ½″ into the plaster, to aid in reassembly of the mold (Figure 217).

7. After the plaster sets, remove the clay wall and soap the edges of the plaster where the new mold sections will come into contact with the completed section (Figure 218). If a retaining shell is required (see Step 8), the surface of the section, which should be smooth, should also be soaped.

8. Repeat the above steps until the mold is completed (Figures 219, 220, 221, and 222). If a great number of sections are involved, it may be necessary to build a retaining shell to hold mold sections in place during reassembly and casting.

Figure 218.

Figure 219.

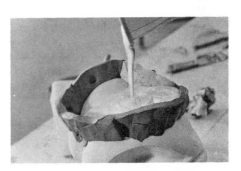

Figure 220.

Figure 221.

Figure 222.

Figure 215.

Figure 216.

Figure 217.

72

Piece Mold (with Retaining Shell)

1. Complete Steps 1-8 for "Piece Mold (Hard Shell)," but do not dimple the clay retaining walls. Be certain to place the model on its side and to divide the mold sections into two groups (dividing the model in half) (Figure 223).

2. Apply a heavy coat of stearine-kerosene solution to the outside faces of the mold sections. Mold soap may also be used.

3. Place clay plugs over the wire loops so that the loops do not become embedded in the plaster of the retaining shell, and to provide an opening in the retaining shell so that the mold sections can be held in place (Figure 224). The clay plugs should stand high enough to protrude through the plaster which is applied to make the retaining shell.

4. Apply a thick coat of plaster to form one half of the shell (Figure 225).

5. Turn the model over, remove the clay walls if any were used, and apply mold separator to the edge of the completed retaining shell which will come into contact with the fresh plaster of the second half of the shell.

6. Repeat Step 4, to form the second half of the retaining shell.

7. Remove the retaining shells, and clean the clay from the holes left by the clay plugs (Figure 226).

8. Remove the mold sections from the model.

9. Replace the mold sections in their proper places in the retaining shell (Figure 227). Mold sections can be held in place by tying wire to the loops on the mold sections, then passing the wire through the corresponding hole in the shell, where it is twisted around a stick placed across the hole (Figure 228).

10. Join and bind the retaining shell containing the mold sections in preparation for casting (Figure 229).

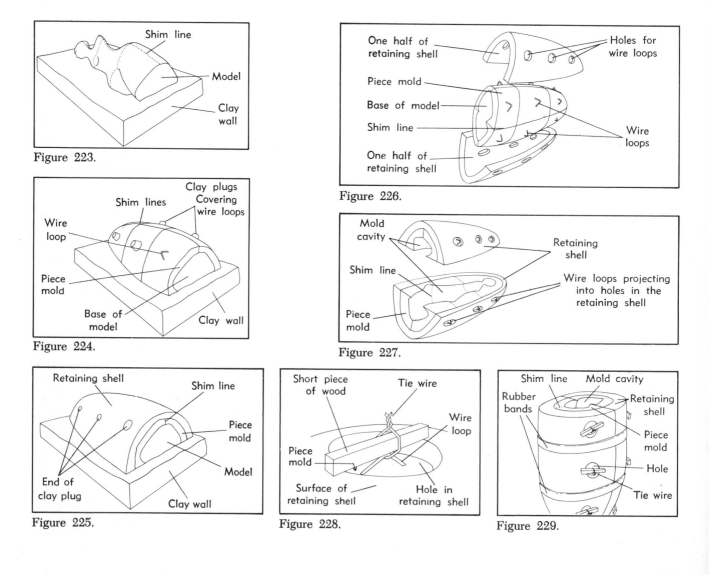

Figure 223.

Figure 224.

Figure 225.

Figure 226.

Figure 227.

Figure 228.

Figure 229.

Figure 230.

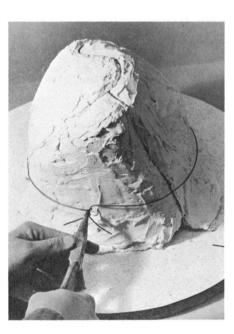

Figure 231.

Figure 232.

Casting a Piece Mold (Solid Cast)

1. Faces and edges of the sections of the mold are treated with the proper mold separator (pages 125-126).
2. The mold is assembled and held together with wire (Figures 230 and 231), heavy rubber bands cut from inner tubes (Figure 232), or metal springs.
3. If necessary, fill the seams with clay on the outside of the mold to prevent the casting medium from leaking out of the mold (Figure 233).
4. Soak the mold with water.
5. Fill the mold; take care to avoid trapping air in the mold during the pour. Rock and vibrate the mold to facilitate the release of air and to force the medium into undercuts. Level the bottom of the cast by drawing a flat stick across the bottom of the mold (Figure 234).
6. After the cast has hardened, remove the sections of the mold from the cast and re-treat the mold with separator in preparation for the next cast. It may be necessary to rap the mold sections or blast with compressed air to release them from the cast.

Figure 233.

Figure 234.

Piece Mold (Hollow Cast)

1. Complete Steps 1-4 for "Piece Mold (Solid Cast)."
2. Pour semi-thick plaster into the mold until it is about half-filled (Figure 235).
3. Roll the mold in such a way as to coat all of the surfaces on the inside of the mold, especially those of the undercuts, if there are any (Figure 236).
4. Pour the plaster out of the mold (Figure 237).
5. Reinforce the inside of the wet plaster cast with fibrous materials such as burlap, straw, or cloth; by pressing the materials gently onto the wet plaster (Figure 238). Do not force the reinforcing materials through the plaster, or they will show on the surface of the cast. If additional reinforcing is necessary allow the first coating to harden before adding a second coating.
6. Repeat Steps 2, 3, and 4 until the desired wall thickness is achieved.
7. Remove the mold, and treat it with a separator in preparation for the next casting.

Figure 235.

Figure 236.

Figure 237.

Figure 238.

Flexible Molds

Flexible molds, being somewhat elastic, permit the casting of complex pieces which have some mild undercutting — without resorting to the use of molds constructed of many sections.

Latex Mold

1. Fasten the model to a base with at least 1″ of free space around the model for flange space.
2. Spray or brush the model with shellac thinned with alcohol (Figure 239).
3. Brush on the first layer of latex (the brush should be stored in soapy water) (Figure 240).
4. Apply folded cheesecloth saturated with latex, as a registration flange (Figures 241 and 242).
5. Undercuts and deep holes must be reinforced with a paste of latex filler, applied in layers 1/16″ thick. This paste can be obtained commercially or made from liquid latex and a filler such as talc or sawdust.
6. Allow the latex to dry until a color change takes place.

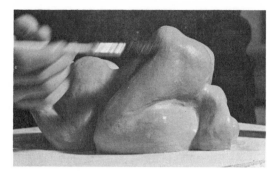

Figure 239.

Figure 240.

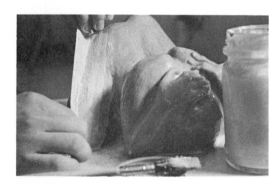

Figure 241.

Figure 242.

7. Repeat 4 or 5 layers, until the required thickness is achieved.

8. The mold is dry when the latex snaps back after being pulled with the fingernail; even so, the mold should cure 48 hours before it is removed from the model.

9. Cut the mold with a razor blade along the registration flange and remove it from the model (Figure 243).

10. If the mold is large and tends to sag, a two-piece plaster shell can be built around the latex mold before it is removed from the model — see "Piece Mold (with Retaining Shell)."

11. Rinse the mold with soapy water before casting.

12. Assemble the mold and fasten it along the registration flange (Figure 244). If the mold has a plaster shell, the mold should not be removed from the shell if possible. The shell containing the mold can be held together with wire, rubber bands, metal spring clamps, and so on.

13. Fill the mold in the usual manner, avoiding trapping air and air bubbles.

14. Open the mold and remove the cast. If the mold is to be stored, it should be cleaned and dusted with talc.

Figure 243.

Figure 244.

CEMENT

Cement and its aggregates should be mixed dry; see directions for mixing cement on page 60. If aggregates are used in the casting, the surface of the dried cast should be rasped, filed, or ground to remove the scum in order to reveal the color and texture of the aggregate. If the cast is not overly complex, the mold can be removed from the cast shortly after the matrix has hardened, and a fine hard spray of water can be directed against the cast to cut the surface scum. This treatment will impart a coarse texture to the cast, and may undesirably soften detail and round edges.

Plaster molds should be treated with two coats of shellac thinned with alcohol, plus a coating of motor oil; or with a heavy application of a solution of mutton tallow and kerosene; or by soaking the mold in a mixture of linseed oil and beeswax for two days, then washing with kerosene — and brushing, immediately before casting, with a thin mix of stearic acid dissolved in kerosene.

Cement casts should not be removed from plaster molds for several days and should be kept soaking wet for the first three days, and damp for the next 25 days to prevent the cement from cracking or crumbling. The cast may be removed for special treatment, but the surface should not be allowed to dry for at least a week. Cement casts should be removed from flexible molds as soon as possible, as the lime in the cement will affect the molds. Latex molds should be treated with green soap as a separator, gelatin molds should be coated with grease.

Pouring the Cement Cast (Piece Mold)

1. Soak the plaster mold in water.
2. Apply the separator.
3. Assemble the mold.
4. Pour or tamp cement into the mold.
5. Vibrate, shake, rock, and puddle the mix (if fluid) to release air. Once the cement begins to stiffen, it must not be disturbed until it has become hard.
6. Keep the mold soaking wet for three days.
7. Remove the cast from the mold for finishing, but keep the cast wet for about 25 more days.

Pouring the Cement Cast (Waste Mold)

1. Plaster molds should be soaked in water before the mold separator is applied and immediately before casting.
2. Treat the mold with the proper separator.
3. Remove excess water with a soft cloth or with blasts of air.
4. Assemble the mold (page 73).

5. Slowly pour the cement into the mold, without splashing. If the mix is too stiff to pour, it must be tamped carefully so that all of the air will be forced out of the cast.
6. If the mix is fluid, shake, vibrate, or rock the mold in order that undercuts fill with cement. Do not disturb the cement after it has begun to harden, or the cast will become fractured.
7. Level the bottom of the cast by drawing a flat stick across the bottom of the mold.

SAND OR CLAY RELIEF MOLDS

Clay and sand molds for relief sculpture are simple to construct and are in extensive use. Clay or damp sand (containing a little clay to serve as a binder) is modeled in a box with a retaining wall about 1½″ higher than the level of the clay or sand (Figure 245). After the model is completed in intaglio or cameo relief, a medium, commonly plaster or cement (metal is discussed on page 92), is allowed to flow slowly over the surface of the model until the box is filled (Figures 246 and 247). After the cast has hard-

Figure 245.

Figure 246.

Figure 247.

ened, the completed relief can be lifted away and additional casts can be made. In the cast of a clay mold, a blast of compressed air may help separate the clay mold from the cast, without the damage that might otherwise occur. It must be remembered that, as in other molding systems, the cast will be in reverse of the mold. If the cast is required in the same pattern as the mold, it will be necessary to make a cast of the original casting, using the first cast as a mold.

CLAY

Clay castings can be created either through the use of a slip (fluid clay) poured into a mold, or through the use of a plastic clay packed into a mold. In either case, an absorbent mold is needed to remove excess water from the clay to make it stiff enough to be self-supporting.

Tools Required

Assorted wood and wire modeling tools (Figure 248.)

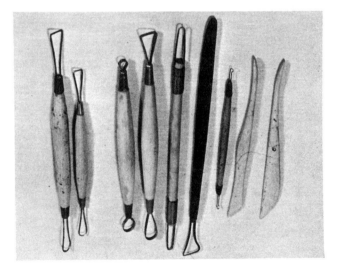

Figure 248.

Slip Casting

1. Construct a plaster piece mold (pages 70-71). Do not use mold separator on the surfaces of the mold, as this will prevent the mold from drawing water from the clay.

2. Allow the mold to dry 3-14 days, depending on the thickness of the mold and the temperature and humidity of the room.

3. Assemble the mold. If the mold is bone-dry, it should be dusted with talcum powder to prevent clay from sticking to the face of the mold (Figures 232 and 233).

4. Prepare the slip (pages 36 and 124).
    a. Slake the clay for an hour or more.
    b. Blunge the slip.
    c. If there is danger of foreign material — twigs, pebbles, nails, or leaves — in the slip, the slip should be passed through a 60-mesh screen.
    d. Allow the slip to age a day or two, then decant excess water which comes to the top.
    e. Blunge the slip to remove air before pouring the cast.

5. Fill the mold with slip, and allow it to stand until a ¼″ to ½″ wall is deposited on the face of the mold. When the surface level of the slip falls, slip should be added to maintain the proper level (Figure 249).

6. Pour the remaining slip out of the mold (Figure 250).

7. Trim the bottom of the mold with a wire tool (Figure 251).

8. Allow the cast to remain in the mold until it shrinks away from the mold (Figure 252).

9. Remove the mold by turning it so that the cast rests on its base; remove the topmost mold sections first.

10. Trim the seams with a wire tool. Use some of the trimmings from the seams to fill small air holes or irregular spots. Wood modeling tools can be used to sharpen detail or to make corrections where necessary, if the tools are not over-used.

11. The process can be repeated until the mold is too wet to absorb water, at which time clay will no longer be deposited on the mold wall. If additional casts are required, the mold must first be dried.

12. Dry and prepare the cast for firing (pages 38-39).

Figure 249.

Figure 250.

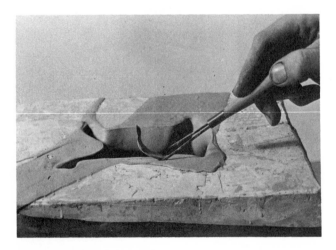

Figure 251.

Figure 252.

Casting with Plastic Clay

1. Construct a piece mold (page 70). Do not use a mold separator on the faces of the mold.
2. Allow the mold to dry for a day or more, depending on the thickness of the mold, the temperature, and the humidity of the area.
3. The mold should not be bone-dry. If it becomes too dry, dampen it with a sponge or spray with a light mist of water.
4. Small balls of plastic clay are pressed firmly onto the face of the mold in such a way that they blend together to form the wall of the cast. Separate sections of the mold can be packed before they are joined to the rest of the mold, but care must be taken to form a ridge of clay around the edges of the mold section so that the clay walls can be easily joined at the seams between the mold sections (Figure 253).
5. After the walls are built up (between ¼″ to ½″) and the clay has stiffened, the cast can be placed on its base and the mold removed.
6. The mold should be trimmed with wire tools and irregularities repaired with wood modeling tools.
7. Allow the cast to dry; prepare the cast for firing (pages 38-39).

Figure 253.

PLASTIC

Plastics that are fluid and can be caused to harden by chemical action or heat, can be used in the casting process. Phenolic resin (Marblette #69*) and polyester resin (Marbl Cast*) are plastics commonly used for this purpose. Piece molds, waste molds, lost wax processes in plaster, and some flexible molds, such as the latex mold, are suited to some plastic casting. The molds are prepared for plastic casting as indicated for plaster on pages 70-71, but different separators are required for plastic. Normally, manufacturer's instructions should be followed if available. For phenolic and polyester resins, plaster molds should be rinsed with polyvinyl alcohol, and given a coat of very thin shellac and two coats of liquid floor wax. Latex molds should be brushed with alcohol, then coated with castor oil.

Some plastics require additional treatment. Marbelette* requires a mold preheated to 150° F., thereby eliminating the use of latex molds. Other plastics, requiring more complex treatment, are impractical for the sculptor.

If aggregates or colorants are to be used in the plastic, they should be thoroughly mixed into the plastic by machine, before the hardening agent or catalyst is added. The hardening agent should also be mixed in by machine.

Because some plastics are thick, they tend to trap air in the mold. Removal of this air can be expedited with vacuum equipment or through centrifugal action.

METAL

Molten metals can be cast in molds of many materials, including salt, ashes, loam, clay, sand, and plaster. The two most common molding substances — recipes of which vary to suit the metal and its pouring temperature — are plaster investment and sand. Because of their divergent natures, each utilizes a different casting system. Plaster investment is usually used in the lost wax method of casting, whereas sand is used in a piece mold technique. Since the qualities of the castings of either system are comparable (dependent primarily on the quality of the molding material and the skill of the foundryman), the casting system selected should be a matter of suitability of the casting system with respect to the problem, the metal, and the capabilities of the foundry being used. Complex forms of small and medium size, and large complex forms which must be cast in sections, are usually cast in investments. Cast iron is almost invariably cast in sand, because most investments cannot stand the extreme heat of molten iron.

---

*Trade name; product of Marblette Corp.

Figure 254. *Toy Warrior on a Horse* (originally on wheels), cast bronze and copper, Delhi area, India, Collection of H. Hasselschwert.

Figure 255. *Rama*, South India, mid 19th century, cast bronze, Collection of H. Hasselschwert.

Lost Wax in Plaster Investment

1. Form the model in sheet or solid wax, or build it up on a core made up of investment (page 42 and Figure 256).
2. Construct the core around a wire armature, if necessary, building to within 1/8″ of the finished size. (Figures 257 and 258.) Receipes for various investments are listed on page 126. In each recipe, mix the crushed dry ingredients before sifting the powder into the water. Luto (investment which has been previously used in the casting process, then crushed) should be screened free of lumps before it is added to the other ingredients. Asbestos fibers may be added to the investment for strength if desired. When using commercial investments such as Non-Ferrous Investment #1 or PVI 10, be certain that the manufacturers' directions are followed exactly. Investments, for the most part, are mixed in the same manner as plaster (page 60), but because investment mixes tend to set quite rapidly, the slurry should be mixed with a power mixer and, if possible, de-aired with vacuum equipment.

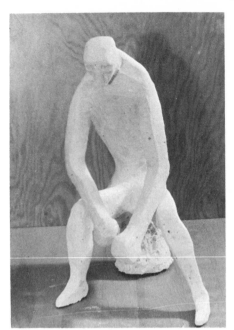

Figure 258.

Figure 256.

Figure 259.

Figure 257.

3. Press warm lumps or strips of wax onto the core in a uniform thickness of about 3/16″. This wax can also be applied by dipping the core into molten wax, or by brushing the wax onto the core with a paint brush (Figure 259).
4. Modify the surface of the wax with any suitable tool. Heated metal can be pressed onto the wax to create textures, or to form planes or lines (Figures 260 and 261). Use sharp implements to scrape or cut the wax surface.
5. Construct a gate of 3/8″ rods of wax (Figures 262, 263, 264, 265, and 323). Attach the solid rods to the model either by pressure or by heating the rod ends and melting them onto the

Figure 260.

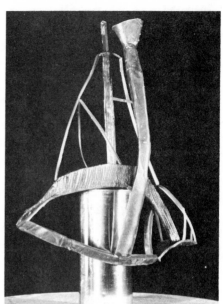

Figure 263.

Figure 261.

Figure 264.

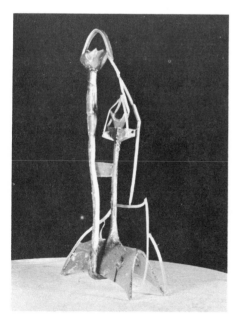

Figure 262.

Figure 265.

model. It is important that the runners leave the sprue at an upward angle and enter the model in the same way (Figures 266 and 323). Applying the runners in any other way may cause turbulence when the metal is poured, causing rough surfaces, freezing and blocking of the passage. The gating system must channel the molten metal to every part of the model in plentiful amounts, or sections of the cast may not receive enough metal to fill the cavity. Risers should be placed in the gating system to store enough extra molten metal so that when the cast begins to cool and shrink, hot metal will flow down from the riser filling the gap left as a result of the shrinking action (Figure 323). Sections of the cast which are lost can sometimes be repaired by brazing the area closed with brazing rod made of a metal similar to the metal of the casting (Figure 267).

6. Attach vents, consisting of ¼″ strips of wax, to the model in such a way that there will be no pockets of air trapped in undercuts, which may block the metal, or cause eruptions of the fluid metal as a result of the sudden violent expansion of the trapped air (Figures 262, 263, and 323). Enough of a venting system must be constructed so that the back pressure of escaping gas is never great enough to restrict the flow of the metal; otherwise, the metal may freeze before the mold is filled.

Figure 267.

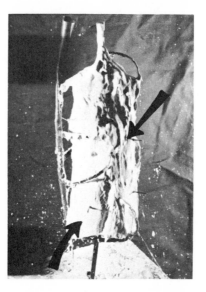

Figure 268.

Figure 266.

Figure 269.

7. Insert metal pins (chaplets) through the wax into the core to prevent the core from shifting when the wax is melted out of the mold (Figures 268, 280, and 323). The pins should be made of a metal with a higher melting point than the pouring point of the metal used for the cast, and should be long enough so that the pins will be firmly embedded in both the core and the mold.

8. Obtain or construct a container large enough to hold the model with its attached gate and risers, plus 3″ of clearance all the way around, 3″ below the model, and even with the top of the pouring basin on the gating system. If the container does not have a bottom, fasten the container to a firm base with clay (Figure 269). Metal or stiff plastic sheets can be coiled and taped to any size desired, if cardboard or plastic containers are not available (Figure 269).

9. Form a cylinder of plaster lath which will clear the container wall by about 1″ and insert it into the container. This mesh will reinforce the plaster when the container is removed or burned away, and it will hold the model in place until the investment has hardened (Figure 270).

10. Spray the model lightly with alcohol on a thin green soap solution to help clean the surface of the wax.

11. Suspend the model in the container by wires fastened to the chaplets and the plaster lath, so that the model will not float or shift when the investment is poured under and around the model. The model should clear the bottom of the container by about 3″.

12. Mix enough investment to fill the container in one pour. If more than one pour must be made to fill the container, probability is great that the layers of the pours will separate during the burnout of the mold, allowing metal to escape from the mold, and preventing the mold from filling. Separating or cracking of the mold will also cause serious flashing on the casting (Figure 271). Flashing is the formation of thin webs of metal projecting out from the surface of the cast.

13. Fill the container while vibrating or rocking it gently to release trapped air and to make positive contact with the surface of the model. Vacuum equipment should be used to exhaust trapped air if possible. The investment should not close the vents or the pouring basin.

14. Remove the container after the investment hardens. Do not attempt to remove the reinforcing wire, even if it is exposed.

Figure 270.

Figure 271.

15. Two to eight hours after the investment hardens, place the flask (the invested model) in a burnout oven or a kiln, which can be a simple firebrick box (Figures 272, 273, and 274). If the wax is to be saved, invert the flask over a trough constructed to catch and drain the wax out of the kiln (Figure 272). If the wax is not to be saved, it can be burned off with the flask right-side-up, in pouring position.

16. Heat the flask to 250° F., until the wax has melted or burned out of the flask. This operation in the case of a small flask, may take 5-8 hours.

17. After the wax is burned out, heat the kiln to 1400° F., until the flask is a dull glowing red. This operation may take up to 48 hours. Do not

Figure 272.

Figure 273.

Figure 274.

attempt to rush or cut short the burn-out. If a blue flame is visible at the pouring basin, all of the wax has not been burned out, even though the flask may appear red hot. The presence of moisture can be detected by the appearance of condensation on a cold metal plate placed at the mouth of the pouring basin.

18. When the flask is a dull glowing red, shut the kiln off and close all of the openings, so the flask will cool slowly, preventing damage to the flask due to uneven contraction.

19. When the flask is cool enough to handle with gloves, remove it from the kiln and embed it in dry sand for pouring (Figures 275 and 276). Prevent sand from entering the gating system.

20. If there is danger of the metal flowing out of the side or bottom of the flask because of a break in the flask or because of separation, ram damp sand tightly around the flask and make the pour immediately.

21. Pour the molten metal directly into the pouring basin in a steady stream, as rapidly as possible, with no splashing. At no time should the metal disappear down the sprue faster than it is poured from the crucible. The pour should not be stopped until the mold is filled, except for reasons of safety or because of obvious failure of

Figure 275.

Figure 276.

the flask; otherwise, the cast will have a series of disconnected layers of metal (Figure 277), or sections of the cast may be blocked by frozen metal.

22. Allow the flask to cool, several hours for a small cast and overnight for a large one. Removal of a hot casting may result in surface cracks or checks. Some metals, like bronze, are brittle at high temperatures and may crumble if disturbed.

23. Remove the investment with picks (Figure 278), knives, light hammers (Figure 279), pointed wires, and similar tools (Figure 280). Save the investment for luto. The light scum on the surface of the cast can be blown off with air or washed away with water.

24. Clean the casting. Bronze castings can be cleaned by brushing the casting with concentrated nitric acid (in open air), then neutralizing with a bath of hot baking soda solution.

Lost Wax in Ceramic Shell Casting

1. Construct the model in a material which will either melt or burn out clean; the traditional medium is wax.

2. Add a gating system with risers and vents. Some shell processes do not require vents, since the shell material is porous enough to allow the air to pass out of the shell through the walls.

3. Dip the model in acetone to remove any trace of grease from the surface.

4. Wash the wax model with an alcohol-shellac solution and allow it to dry (Figure 281).

5. Dip the model in a freshly stirred slurry (a suspension of silicon refractory flour and a binder-like hydrolyzed ethyl silicate) to form an even covering. If cracks are found, wash the slurry

Figure 279.

Figure 280.

Figure 277.

Figure 278.

Figure 281.

from the model with water, and repeat the dipping action until an even coat is achieved (Figure 282).

6. Coat the slurry with stucco (an air-floated refractory grog) by blowing the stucco over the wet slurry (Figure 283).

7. Repeat the coating until a ¼″ wall, or larger, is built up.

8. Invert the shell and insert it in an oven preheated to the melting temperature of the wax. The shell must be brought to heat quickly to prevent the expansion of the wax from cracking the shell. Infrared lamps can be used effectively.

9. Fire the shell for 4 hours at 1300° F., to burn out the residue.

10. Pack the shell in sand preheated at 500° F., to prevent thermal shock and the hydraulic force of the heated metal from rupturing the shell. The sand can be worked tightly around the shell by vibrating the container in which the sand and shell are placed.

11. Pour the metal into the still-hot shell.

12. The shell can be removed from the casting with a hot chemical bath, but if this commercial service is not available it can be broken loose with hand tools, wire brushes, or sandblasting equipment.

Lost Wax in Piece Mold

1. Treat the model with mold separator (pages 125-126).

2. Attach a wax gating and venting system to the model (Figure 284).

3. Make a piece mold of the model, using investment instead of plaster. Do not coat the piece mold with mold separator. When the mold is removed from the model, the venting and gating system should break away from the model and remain buried within the piece mold. Clean the faces of the mold.

4. Coat the inside faces of the piece mold with an even layer of wax between 1/8″ and 3/16″ thick, depending on the size of the cast (Figure 285).

5. Assemble the piece mold, and wrap wire around the outside of the mold to hold it together. When the mold is assembled, these wax layers should be joined at the edges of the mold sections with wax, in order to form a continuous wax layer over the face of the mold.

6. Drill holes through the investment and the wax, and insert chaplets, so that the chaplets will bind the core which is yet to be poured, to the shell of the mold (Figure 286).

7. Soak the piece mold in water.

8. Place the mold in a container as in Steps 8 and 9 (page 83).

Figure 282.

Figure 283.

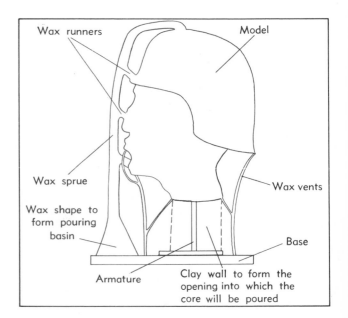

Figure 284.

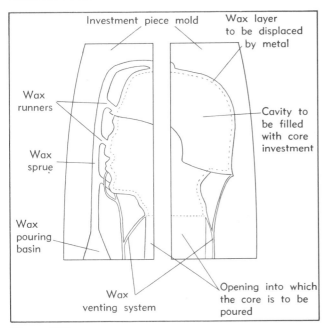

Figure 285.

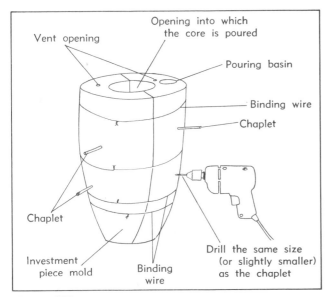

Figure 286.

9. Mix and pour an investment into the container, around and under the mold, and fill the cavity in the mold which will become the core of the piece mold. Do not cover the pouring basin or the vents of the gating system.

10. Remove the container, burn out the mold, bury it in sand, and make the pour (Steps 13-24, pages 83-85).

Sand Casting

Sand Casting Tools

a. Snap flask drag (Figure 287); with cope (Figure 288); and assembled snap flask (Figure 289)

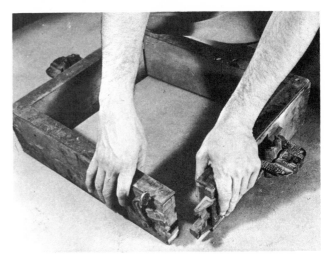

Figure 287.

Figure 288.

Figure 289.

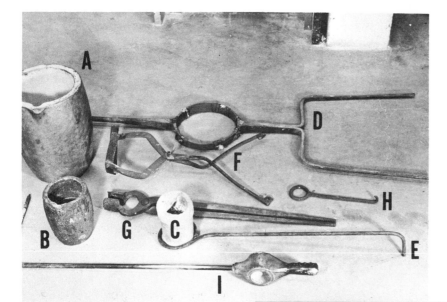

Figure 290.

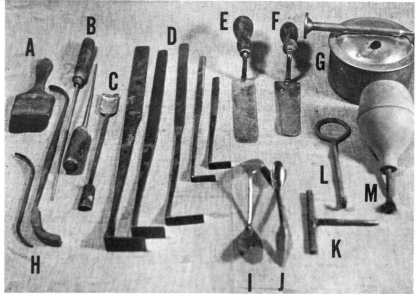

Figure 291.

Figure 292.

b. Crucibles (Figures 290A, 290B, and 290C)
c. Pouring shank, 2-man (Figure 290D)
d. Pouring shank, 1-man (Figure 290E)
e. Bent handle crucible tongs (Figure 290F)
f. Straight handle crucible tongs (Figure 290G)
g. Hook for lifting lid (Figure 290H)
h. Pyrometer (Figure 290I)
i. Molder's brush (Figure 291A)
j. Venting wires (Figures 291B)
k. Runner tool (Figure 291C)
l. Set of bench lifters (Figure 291D)
m. Square trowel (Figure 291E)
n. Tapered trowel (Figure 291F)
o. Mouth spray can (Figure 291G)
p. Gating tools and spoon (Figure 291H)
q. Slick and oval spoon (Figure 291I)
r. Gate cutter and spoon (Figure 291J)
s. "T" draw screw (Figure 291K)
t. Bulb sponge (Figure 291L)
u. Hook to lift hot castings (Figure 291M)
v. Sprue or riser pins (Figure 292A)
w. Rammers (Figure 292B)
x. Bench rammer with peen (Figure 292C)
y. Ingot pattern (Figure 292D)
z. Riddle (Figure 293C)

Other Tools

Tools that are required for maintaining the condition of the sand, but are not illustrated, are a square shovel, a rake, and a sprinkling can. Additional tools which will be valuable for sand casting include a molder's bellows (Figure 293B) and a laddle for dipping small amounts of metal from the crucible for small pours (Figure 293A).

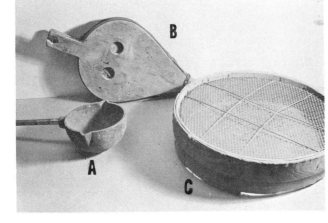

Figure 293.

Casting a Pattern

1. The model, if wood, plaster, cement, or porous metal, is given two coats of shellac diluted with alcohol, then dusted with parting (a commercial parting compound). The parting is kept in a cloth bag which is simply shaken over the pattern to deposit a light film of the white dust.
2. Mark the model to determine the divisions which will present no undercutting.
3. Ram the bottom half of the flask (drag) full of sand (Figures 294 and 295), and draw a straight edge across the top of the drag to produce a level surface (Figure 296). The sand should be just damp enough to lump together when squeezed in the hand and to leave a crisp edge when the lump is broken in half.
4. Hollow an area a little larger than the model, in the sand (Figure 297), then riddle (shake sand through a screen high above the flask) sand into the hollow (Figure 298).
5. Press the model into the sand to form one-half of the mold (Figure 299). Ram all of the surrounding sand level (Figure 300).
6. Sprinkle parting over the sand and model (Figure 301).
7. Fit the top of the flask (cope) over the drag so that the cope is held in alignment by the pins which fit in the lugs (Figure 302).
8. Insert a gate pin into the sand of the drag. This pin must stand higher than the top of the cope.
9. Riddle and ram sand into the cope until the cope is filled. Carve a pouring basin in the sand around the gate pin (Figure 303).
10. Strike the gate pin a light blow on the side and lift it out with a slight twisting motion.
11. Lift the cope from the drag (Figure 304).
12. Tap the model to loosen it, then remove it from the sand (Figure 305). On large patterns, screw the "T" draw screw into the pattern, rap on the screw lightly from side to side, then lift the pattern out by the "T" handle.
13. Carve a groove (runner) in the sand to carry the molten metal to the cavity caused by the removal of the model (Figure 306). Blow loose sand from the drage with a bellows.
14. If the sand becomes too dry at any point, spray a fine mist of water on the sand with an atomizer or the mouth spray can.
15. If a smooth surface is desired, spray a mixture of graphite and molasses on the mold surface, and dry it with a torch or in an oven. Molds for steel or iron should be sprayed with a mixture of powdered silica, molasses, and water.

Figure 294.

Figure 295.

Figure 296.

Figure 297.

Figure 298.

Figure 299.

Figure 300.

Figure 301.

Figure 302.

Figure 303.

Figure 304.

Figure 305.

Figure 306.

16. Replace the cope on the drag (Figure 306), and weight the sand with heavy slabs of metal to prevent the sand from floating on top of the heavy molten metal.
17. Pour the molten metal into the pouring basin as smoothly and quickly as is practical.
18. Shake or vibrate the sand from the model after the casting has cooled enough to be handled. Commercial castings are often sandblasted to clean the surfaces that may have a great deal of scale.

Models which have undercuts or are hollow require additional steps. Cores can be made by making a plaster mold of the model, packing the mold with sand that has been mixed with boiled linseed oil (page 126), all of which is then baked at 450° F. to harden the core. After the hardened core is removed from the mold, a layer of the surface of the core is filed away, in a thickness equal to the desired thickness of the cast — between 1/8" and 3/16", depending on the size of the model. Cores are held in place with chaplets (Figure 307). Undercuts can be handled by building up removable sections of sand in a manner similar to piece molding. Sand used for these removable sections should be mixed with a solution of gelatinized starch, dextrin and molasses (page 126), so that the sections will become hard

Figure 307.

enough to handle after drying a short time. During construction, the sections should be isolated from the other sand with parting; cores and removable sections may absorb moisture from the surrounding sand and lose strength, if left in place too long, resulting in casting failures. Pours should be made as quickly as possible after the mold is assembled.

Sand Casting by Direct Displacement

Dry materials or objects which are able to vaporize with comparably small volumes of gas, such as ping-pong balls, corrugated cardboard, balloons, straw, or styroform*, can be shaped and assembled in any desired manner, embedded in sand, and cast direct. The molten metal vaporizes the material, and the gasses formed pass into the sand, allowing the metal to fill the cavity just formed.

1. Riddle a layer of sand into a box.
2. Pack the bottom of the model with sand, and place the model in the bottom of the box, bottom down (Figure 308).
3. Place a gate pin adjacent to the model or attach a styrofoam runner to the model and to the gate pin (Figure 309).
4. Riddle and ram sand over the model, filling the box (Figure 310).
5. Rap and remove the gate pin.
6. If the casting is large, repeatedly drive a thin wire through the sand to help vent excess gas which may be formed.
7. Weight the top of the sand, then pour the metal. Metal poured directly over embedded materials must have enough heat to vaporize the volatile pattern. Molten lead does not have sufficient heat to vaporize materials commonly used for direct casting, whereas molten iron, given time, will displace most volatile materials. There is some danger inherent in the use of these materials, as it is possible that violent expansion of the gasses of the materials may blow the molten metal back out of the sand.

Sand Casting (Direct Carving)

Sand which has a good binder can be carved to form original one-time molds. Bulky casts attained through this process are usually excessively heavy, so the process is primarily restricted to relief sculpture. If an inch or so of thickness of metal is not prohibitive, an open-face casting can be executed, but open-face castings are heavy, expensive (because of the waste metal), and they do not always receive a good impression on the casting. Closed-face casting, on

---

*Casting in this manner was patented by Harold F. Shroyer in April of 1953, and eventually licensed to the Full Mold Process Co., Lathrop Village, Mich.

Figure 308.

Figure 309.

Figure 310.

the other hand, gives fine impressions on the cast, is lighter than open-face casting, and is therefore less expensive. Closed-face castings are more time consuming and more difficult to produce than open-face castings, however.

Sand Casting (Direct Carving, Open Face)

1. Riddle and ram sand into a box.
2. Strike off the sand to form a level surface.
3. Carve the appropriate design in the sand, in reverse. High points on the desired cast must be deep points in the carved sand. Lettering and similar devices must be carved in the sand to read backwards.
4. Pour molten metal into the design.

Sand Casting (Direct Carving, Closed Face)

1. Riddle and ram sand in a drag (Figure 311).
2. Strike off the sand (form a level surface) (Figure 312).
3. Carve the design in the sand in reverse (Figures 313-314). Include a gate and runner (Figure 314).
4. Riddle and ram sand in a cope, and strike it off.
5. Cut a sprue hole in the cope sand with a sprue cutter or a piece of thin wall pipe (Figure 315), so that the sprue hole will be directly above the gate carved in the sand of the drag when the cope is placed on the drag.

Figure 313.

Figure 314.

Figure 311.

Figure 312.

Figure 315.

6. Place the cope on the drag (Figure 316).

7. Carve a pouring basin, being careful not to allow sand to fall into the sprue hole (Figure 317). If necessary, the cope can be removed for this operation, or for cleaning out sand that may have fallen into the hole.

8. Weight the sand in the cope, and make the pour.

9. Allow the cast to cool before removing the sand from the casting.

Finishing Metal Castings

After the cast has cooled, the investment or sand is cleaned away (Figures 278, 279, 280, and 318). Sand hardened with artificial binders should be discarded. Investment should be saved for luto. The gating system must be removed by sawing through the vents and risers about ⅛" away from the surface of the sculpture. The ⅛" protrusions are then worked flush with the surface by chasing — lightly striking the nipple with a hammer and punch (Figures 319, 320, and 321). Flashing should be ground to with 1/32" of the surface, then blended in with files and chased with textured punches (Figure 322).

The chaplets should be pulled or drilled out of the metal, the holes tapped, and a threaded wire of metal similar to the cast screwed into place, cut off, and chased.

The metal should then be cleaned with an acid cleaner (page 130), and, if desired, given a patina (pages 130-135).

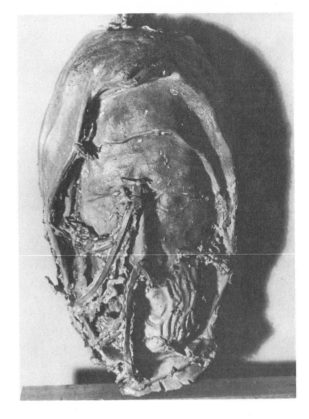

Figure 318.

Figure 316.

Figure 317.

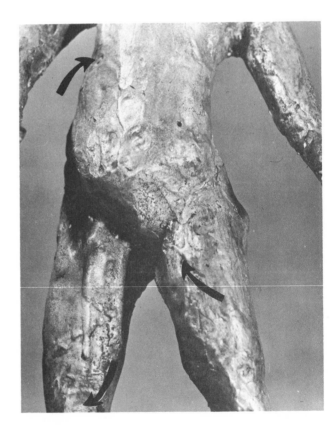

Figure 319.

Figure 320.

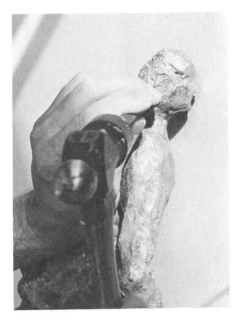

Figure 321.

Figure 322.

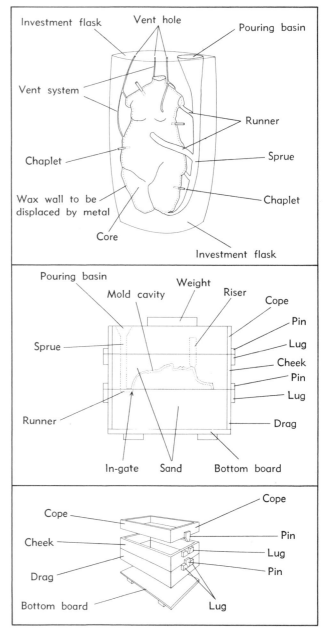

Figure 323.

Melting Metals

Not all metals are suitable for sculptural castings; many are rendered unsatisfactory because of their sluggishness while in a fluid state, some are unsatisfactory because of their excessive rate of contraction (leading to fracturing of the cast), others because they will not take a surface impression, and so on.

Metals which cast well do not always lend themselves to traditional patina techniques, but their ease of casting may offset this difficulty. Some good-to-excellent casting alloys, and their recipes, follow on next page with some additional notes.

METAL	COMPOSITION (PERCENTAGES)	CASTING QUALITY
Yellow Brass	copper, 70; zinc, 25; lead, 3; tin, 2	good
Red brass	copper, 85; zinc, 5; lead, 5; tin, 5	good for sand casting; pour at 2100° F.
Bell bronze	copper, 75; tin, 25	good for sand casting; should be quenched in water (cold) to gain tonal quality
Soft bronze	copper, 88; tin, 12	good
Gun metal	copper, 88; tin, 10; zinc, 2	excellent; pour between 2050° F. and 2200°F.
Phosphor bronze	copper, 88; tin, 11; phosphorus, 1	excellent
Aluminum	any aluminum alloy, preferably without iron or silicon content, pour at as low a temperature as possible	excellent; pour below 1300° F.
Iron		excellent; pour between 2600° F. and 2850° F.
Lead	this metal, out of alloy, normally too soft for sculptural castings; should be alloyed with tin, zinc, or antimony	good; cast at about 630° F.
Cadmium alloys	low-melting alloys of cadmium, lead, and bismuth can be melted on an ordinary gas stove; melting points are often lower than the boiling point of water.	excellent; pouring temperature can range as low as 140° F.

The most inexpensive, and probably the most common, furnace in use for melting non-ferrous metal on a noncommercial basis is the centrifugal furnace, illustrated in Figure 324. In this furnace the crucible rests on a firebrick on the bottom of the furnace, while the flames whirl around the crucible and up to a hole in the lid. Hot gasses pass through the hole in the lid and out an overhead vent. Although the flame is primarily contained within the refractory, proper adjustment of the gas and air mixture will allow the faintest trace of greenish flame to appear at the hole in the lid.

The crucible should be dry and slowly preheated to 250°F. before it is placed in the cold furnace and charged with metal. The centrifugal furnace illustrated in Figure 324 is started by placing a burning oily rag bound to a wire, into the furnace near the gas nozzle, closing the air intake, turning on the centrifugal blower, and opening the gas valve. Once there is a flame in the pit, the air intake is slowly opened to achieve the proper flame. The lid is then placed on the furnace (do not attempt to light this furnace with the lid in place, as an explosion may result), and the flame re-adjusted. The flame will require constant attention, in that its properties change as the temperature in the furnace increases. Various furnaces are lighted in different ways; where possible, manufacturer's directions should be followed to the letter.

When the metal has reached its required fluid temperature, usually 100° F. or more above the pouring temperature, the air valve, the gas valve, and

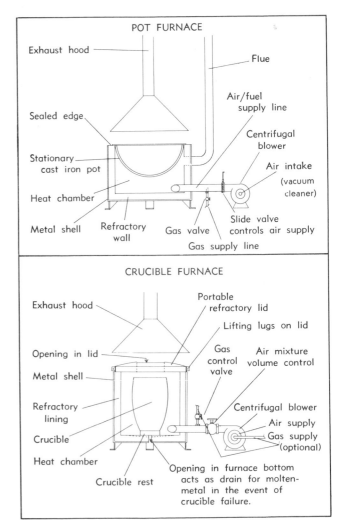

Figure 324.

the blower are turned off — in that order. When neces-sary, fluxes and degassers are usually added at this time — by gently plunging them into the molten metal.

The lid is then removed and put aside, and the crucible lifted out with tongs and placed in a pouring shank, which is resting on a bed of sand. The dross is skimmed from the metal, and when the metal has cooled to its pouring temperature (and tested with a pyrometer), it is poured into the mold (Figure 325).

Aluminum and pot metal (white metal), can be melted in a melting pot furnace, as illustrated in Figure 324. The crucible (in this case, cast iron) is not removed from this furnace; instead, the molten metal is dipped from the pot and poured from a ladle. While aluminum, lead, white metals, and many other low-melting alloys can be melted in cast-iron pots (such as glue pots or old iron kettles), other metals requiring greater heat should be melted in graphite or silicon carbide crucibles.

Figure 325.

CHAPTER 7

Addition

Because the additive method of producing sculpture can have the advantages of freedom from structural limitations, manipulative intimacy, and comparative rapidity of execution, the technique is probably the one most used today. In general, the sculptor utilizes materials which are temporarily fluid, at least in part. In the case of plaster, cement, and certain plastics, the medium is fluid until chemical action or evaporation causes the materials to become rigid. Welded, brazed, or soldered metals, on the other hand, require the use of heat to soften the material to a point suitable for manipulation, after which the metal again freezes. Although some media, like wood and certain plastics, are rigid rather than fluid during the creative process, they may be joined through the use of rivets, screws, nails, glue, or even lock joints; they are, therefore, legitimate media of the additive technique.

Figure 326. *Giraffe,* student work, built-up plaster.

Figure 327. *Emu,* student work, built-up plaster.

Figure 328. Windblown figure I, L. E. Moll, American.

Figure 329. *Language Teacher,* built-up plaster, oil patina.

PLASTER AND CEMENT

Neither plaster nor cement have enough innate strength to retain a shape or position forced on them while in their fluid state, and it is necessary to devise supporting systems known as armatures (pages 31-35) to support these materials. An armature should be strong enough to easily support the full weight of the applied medium without sagging; it should also be rigid enough that it will not flex, vibrate, or sway — thereby causing the material to crack, crumble, or fall off. For small light sculpture, an armature of heavy wire will be adequate. If the sculpture is bulky, a core can be formed by wrapping the wire armature tightly with cheesecloth strips soaked in cement or plaster.

Larger sculpture may require an armature made of iron pipe or welded rods. In such cases, the bulk of the sculpture may be formed by shaping plaster lath to within ¼″ of the desired shape, and wiring this support to the armature.

Styrofoam blocks, fastened together with long wooden or metal pins and glue, and then carved to the desired shape, can be used as an armature (page 34). The face of the styrofoam should be rough so that the medium will have a surface which it can grip.

Tools Required

a. A small flexible mixing container such as half of a rubber ball, or a plastic bowl (Figure 330A)
b. Shellac (Figure 330B)
c. A wire brush for cleaning tools (Figure 330C)
d. Paint brushes (Figure 330D)
e. Spatula (Figure 330E)
f. Sponge (Figure 330F)

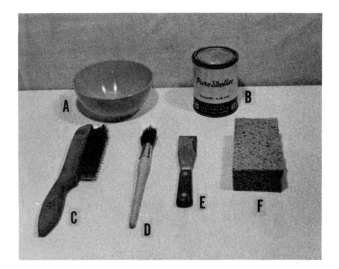

Figure 330.

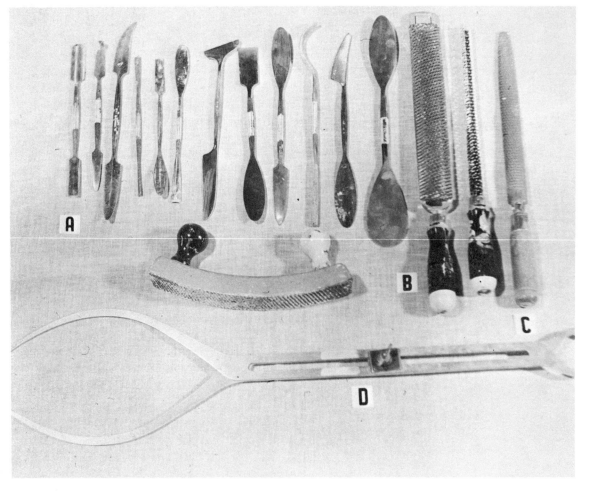

Figure 331.

g. Hot wire cutter or small soldering iron, for cutting styrofoam (Figure 86 and 404).
h. A series of plaster knives and rifflers (Figure 331A)
i. SURFORM® tools (Figure 331B) Stanley Tools Div. of the ST Works, New Brittian, Coon.
j. Rasps (Figure 331C)
k. Proportional dividers (Figure 331D)

Care of Tools

Neither plaster nor cement should be poured down drains. Waste material should be dumped into containers for disposal; rinsing in buckets of water will catch the medium remaining on the hands and in the mixing bowl. Mixing bowls should always be thoroughly cleaned before mixing new batches of medium. Flexible containers can often be peeled off of large masses of hardened material; thin layers will flake away from the sides of the container when it is flexed. Brushes used in shellac can be cleaned with alcohol, even if the shellac has hardened in the brush.

Tools should be cleaned immediately after use, and all metal tools should be dried and oiled to pre-

vent serious rusting. Rifflers, rasps, and SURFORM® tools will work best on plaster which is completely dry; working damp plaster will cause most of these tools to clog, sometimes beyond easy repair. These tools work well on soft aggregate cement, but the harder aggregates — containing high percentages of hard sand or marble chips — will quickly dull them. Clogged tools should be wire-brushed to remove embedded medium, then oiled to prevent rust.

Worn rifflers and rasps can be dipped into liquid epoxy cement, then rolled in carborundum powder or titanium oxide powder of any desired grit, to restore the abrasive character of the tool. The epoxy will cause the grit to adhere to the tool until the grit is worn beyond use, at which time the tool can be recharged by repeating the process.

Plasters and cements should be stored in dampproof containers, preferably fiber drums with plastic bag liners, which can be sealed. Material which is left exposed will eventually absorb moisture from the air, making the cement or plaster useless.

Built-up Plaster

1. Build the armature and fasten it to a solid base (Figure 332).
2. Shellac the armature if it can rust.
3. Mix a thick batch of plaster and apply it in thin layers with a spatula (Figure 333).
4. Mix additional batches and apply them in thin layers with a spatula until the desired form and texture is developed (Figures 334-336).
5. If the build-up process is delayed for more than eight hours, the sculpture should be thoroughly soaked with water to prevent the old plaster on the sculpture from ruining new plaster by absorbing water from the fresh batch.
6. Use plaster knives or similar tools to remove over-building.
7. Allow the plaster to dry after the desired form is achieved.
8. Use rifflers, rasps, files, and, if necessary, sand-paper to refine areas of the sculpture.

Figure 334.

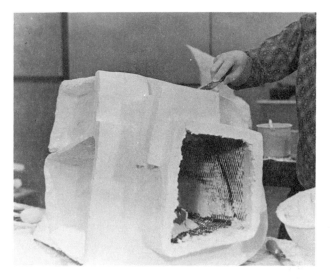

Figure 335.

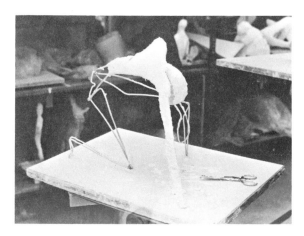

Figure 332.

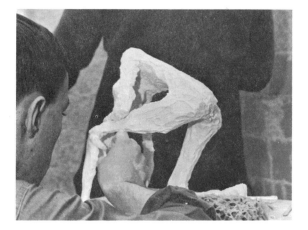

Figure 333.

Figure 336.

Finishing Plaster

The finishes that can be effected on plaster are almost numberless. Raw plaster, polished plaster, transparent or opaque, water-base or oil-base, metal plating (copper, bronze, gold, silver, and steel), or even plastic or rubber surfacing are a few of the finishes available for the medium (pages 128 and 135). Raw plaster has a dead-white, porous surface that attracts dirt and makes the sculpture hard to see. If the whiteness of the plaster is desirable, the surface can be sealed with a clear plastic or wax to prevent the absorption of dirt. Most often, color is applied to soften the harsh appearance of the plaster and to emphasize the surface qualities of the sculpture. Frequently, although incessantly criticized as being false to the medium, the patina on plaster is made to resemble, or to imitate, other media. Commercially, the most common technique for disguising plaster is metal plating. Critics object to this imitation of metal sculpture, but supporters of such processes state that there is no significant difference between the artificial oxidation of bronze to eliminate its natural bright and shiny yellow surface and the plating or painting of plaster to eliminate its natural dull and harsh white surface. Either process results in an artificial treatment of a surface to change or eliminate unwanted characteristics of a medium.

Cement

Cement is built up in much the same manner as plaster, but more time is required for cement to harden than for plaster. A good recipe for the foundation or supporting cement is three parts cement to one part lime putty, by volume. Mortars commonly used for surface build-up have a composition approximating one part Portland cement (white or gray) and

Figure 338. *Bird Watcher,* Harold Hasselschwert, American (1930-   ), cement and steel.

Figure 337. *Growth Forms,* concrete, steel, wood, and ceramic.

three parts fine aggregate (plaster sand, marble dust, marble chips, granite chips, or ground glass), by volume. Concrete is difficult to use for the additive method, because concrete mixes contain large particles of aggregate which resist application in thin layers, especially for a finishing coat. A typical concrete composition is two parts Portland cement, one part perlite (or sand), and one part zonalite (or gravel), by volume. Other recipes are listed on page 126.

Built-up Cement

1. Build a strong armature and fasten it to a solid base. The armature should have a rough surface, such as is provided by plaster lath, so that the cement will have a gripping surface.

2. Paint the armature with shellac if it will rust or otherwise be affected by the lime or water in the cement.

3. Dry mix the powdered ingredients of the cement, including dry pigments if any are to be used.

4. Add water, a little at a time, and fold it into the powder until a slurry, about the consistency of thick rolled oats, is obtained.

5. Apply the matrix in layers about ½″ thick. Score or roughen the surface of the layers if additional layers of cement are to be applied.

6. Allow the first layers to harden 8-10 hours before applying additional layers.

7. Do not allow the cement to dry, at any time, for at least 20 days. Wet cloths and plastic can be wrapped around the sculpture to prevent premature drying.

8. The surface can be rasped 4-10 hours after application, depending on the aggregate. Eventually, after two or three days, stone tools can be used to alter the surface. If aggregates such as perlite or zonalite are used, the cement will usually remain soft enough to be worked with ordinary rasps and chisels.

9. It may be necessary to sand or grind the dry surface of the sculpture to remove the scum of the cement, in order to expose the texture of the aggregate (Figure 173). In some instances, a fine, hard spray of water can be played on the cement which has just hardened, to remove the scum.

10. If coloration is not to be added by the capillary process, the finished sculpture should be washed down with muriatic acid (The commercial preparation for cleaning brick and cement) and then neautralized with water, prior to finishing.

Finishing Cement

Cement should not be treated for the first 28 days except with water. After that period, it can be dried and sealed with commercial cement sealers designed for that purpose. Powdered color can be added to the cement for special effects while it is being mixed. Too much pigment (over 10%), or the wrong kind of pigment, such as tempera pigments, may destroy the cement, or the colorants may be bleached out by the lime in the cement. Commercial colorants, which are safe to use, are available for both cement and plaster.

Cement sculpture which is to be left out-of-doors should be sealed (including the bottom) with three coats of a hot mixture of three parts boiled linseed oil to one part turpentine, by volume. This mixture tends to turn the cement a mellow yellow, and is good for about two years, at which time the treatment should be repeated. Commercial cement floor sealers can also be used — with varying results, depending on the recipe of the cement. Ordinary oil paint can be added to the linseed oil if color is desired on the cement.

Cement can also be colored by capillary action. After the cement is several days old (preferably much older), it can be immersed in solutions of aniline colors, copper sulfate, iron sulfate, and other metallic colors. When the cement has absorbed all of the color that its pores will hold, it becomes somewhat waterproof; if metallic colors are used, the concrete can be buffed and polished to a dull lustre. Upon oxidization, the colors will impart a metallic appearance to the cement.

CLAY

The obvious manner in which to build up a bulk for clay sculpture is to press small lumps of clay onto a large firm clay mass in such a way that the form desired is developed. At this point, modeling is utilized to clarify the form. Over-building should be avoided, but if it does occur, large chunks of clay can be torn away from the mass and the build-up process repeated. This method of building clay can present difficulties if the finished work is to be hollowed and fired. Building with small lumps of clay can form air pockets which may cause the sculpture to explode in the kiln; care must be exercised to avoid this.

Coil Construction

Sculpture constructed by the coil method requires that a fairly complete image of the completed sculpture be fixed in the mind of the artist before the build-up is begun, because the overall form is established from the bottom to the top of the sculpture, without recourse to other than very minor modification (Figures 339, 340). Surface detail can be changed easily, but in coil sculpture the basic form is comparatively unyielding.

1. Wedge a clay mass (pages (37-38).
2. Form lemon-size balls of clay (Figure 341).
3. Roll the clay balls on a dampened cloth until long rolls of clay, about 5/8″ to 3/4″ in diameter, are formed (Figure 342).
4. Lay the first roll of clay on a base to form the bottom of the sculpture (Figure 343). If the sculpture is large, webs of clay should be built up across the inside of the sculpture at the same time that the outside walls are being coiled up. If a coil is not long enough, additional lengths can be slipped on.

Figure 341.

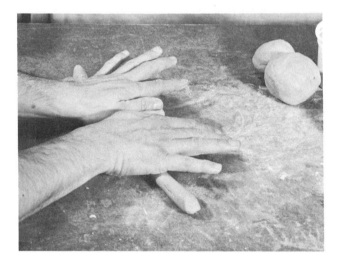

Figure 342.

Figure 339. Primitive ceramic clay pot.

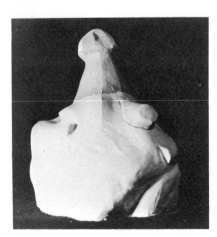

Figure 340.

Woman, coarse ceramic clay and thick white mat glaze.

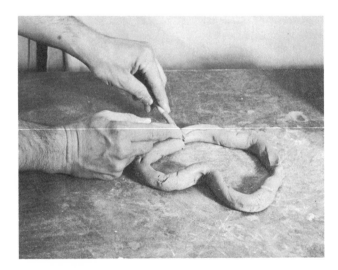

Figure 343.

Figure 344.

Figure 345.

Figure 346.

Figure 347.

5. Serrate the coil along the top with a knife or wire tool (Figure 344), and coat the serrations of the coil with a thick slip. Try to prevent the slip from coating the clay which will be the face of the sculpture, to prevent a slimy or greasy appearance on the surface.

6. Serrate another coil along what will be its bottom, coat the serrations with slip, and lay the coil on top of the first rope of clay (Figure 345). The form of the sculpture is created by varying the position of the coils as they are placed one on top of the other (Figures 346, 347, and 348).

7. Continue to build, coil on coil, forming the shape and size desired (Figures 346, 347, 348, and 349).

8. Blend and texture the surface of the clay with the fingers or clay tools until the desired visual effect is completed (Figure 349). Avoid wetting the surface of the clay as a means of smoothing — this usually leads to unpleasant textural characteristics.

9. Allow the clay to dry slowly, then prepare it for firing (pages 38-39).

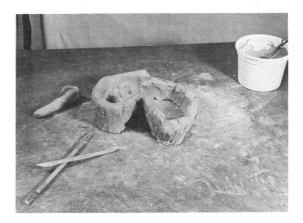

Figure 348.

Figure 349.

Because plastic clay will not support great weight, it may be necessary to allow the bottom coils to dry and become stiff or leather hard before building the sculpture to its full bulk. If this is the case, the modeling of the lower sections of the sculpture should be pretty well completed before the upper sections are ever formed (Figures 350 and 351). If the clay tends to dry too fast (causing cracking), sheet plastic can be wrapped around it to slow the drying time; in extreme cases, a fine film of water may be blown over the clay before covering it. When the sculpture is completed, it should be allowed to dry as slowly· as possible, a procedure which may take weeks.

Slab Construction

1. Wedge the clay (pages 37-38).
2. Roll out a slab of clay on a damp cloth using two 3/8″ square sticks as rails for a rolling pin (Figure 352). Interesting texture can be obtained by varying the kind and coarseness of the cloth on which the clay is rolled.
3. Cut shapes out of the clay with a paring knife or some similar tool (Figure 353).
4. Serrate the edges of the shapes where they are to be joined (Figure 354), coat these serrations with slip (Figure 355), and press the joints together firmly (Figure 356). If desired, the edges can be blended together with modeling tools (Figure 357) or with the fingers.
5. The slabs can be shaped to some extent before they are joined (Figure 355). If the clay is too dry, too coarse, or is stretched too far, it may crack (Figure 358).
6. If the slabs tend to sag, they are too wet and should be permitted to dry a little. If the clay tends to dry too fast, it should be covered with plastic sheets.
7. After the sculpture is completed, dry it as slowly as possible in preparation for firing (pages 38-39).

Figure 351.

Figure 352.

Figure 353.

Figure 350.

Figure 354.

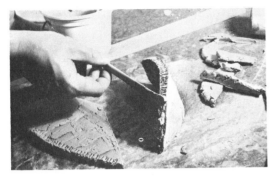

Figure 355.

Figure 356.

Figure 357.

Figure 358.

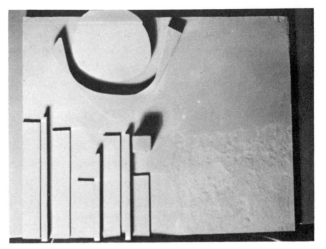

Figure 359A. *City Scape,* painted wood relief.

Figure 359B. *Wood Construction,* red elm.

WOOD

The usual joining methods employed when using wood in an additive manner are nailing, screwing, doweling, gluing, and interlocking. Because of the rigidity of the individual blocks of wood, and the interference with the spontaneous creative process caused by the mechanical nature of joining wood, the additive process is usually de-emphasized and carving a subtractive technique predominates. Wood can be shaped by cutting, grinding, or bending, either before or after the build-up process has taken place.

Nailing is an inferior joining device. It does not pull the separate pieces together; it primarily prevents side movement. Friction prevents the nail from slipping out of the wood or the wood from slipping off the nail. If more than one nail is used, at slight angles towards each other (toe nailing), the point will be significantly stronger — but the pieces of wood will still not be pulled together by the nails. Unless pilot holes are drilled, with a drill slightly smaller than the nail, there is great danger that the nail will split the wood.

A screw joint is one in which a threaded pin pulls the pieces of wood together, and prevents side motion as well, though occasionally a single screw will allow one of the pieces of wood to rotate off of the screw until it is also glued, doweled, nailed, or otherwise prevented from turning. Screw joints are the strongest and most common joints used in woodworking. The screw head can usually be countersunk and the resulting hole plunged with a dowel and glue.

Doweling is the process of pinning a joint with a short wooden shaft which is usually glued into a snug hole in the joint. The hole is drilled through one piece of wood into the second piece of wood (through the joint); then the proper size dowel (preferably fluted) is swabbed with glue and driven into the glue-swabbed hole with a wooden mallet. The dowel can be driven below the surface of the wood and a plug inserted to hide the dowel. When the glue is dry, the dowel and glue will prevent movement of the pieces of wood in any direction. Some sculptural devices utilize the dowel without glue, so that the sculpture can be rearranged at will; as in Figures 360-365.

Figure 361.

Figure 362.

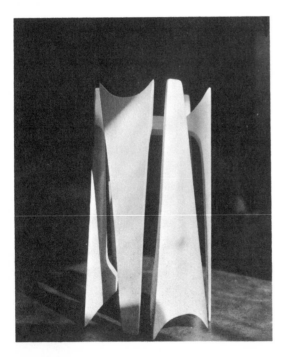

Figure 360.

Figure 363.

Figure 364.

Figure 365.

Joints in wood that are only glued seldom have great strength. Though the glue might hold, the joint may fail under stress, because the wood adjacent to the glue often breaks away, and a paper-thin layer of it will be found stuck to the glue. For joints where there is neither great stress nor great impact, most ordinary wood glues are adequate. For joints where there may be weight, stress, or impact, screws, dowels, or interlocking joints should be used to bear the brunt of leverage, torque, or sheer forces across the face of the joint. Of the many glues available, animal or hide glues have long been favorites, though some require the use of heat and pressure and have long curing times. Newer glues such as the whiteglues (polyvinyl acetate resin), resorcinals, and epoxies are proving satisfactory, if not vastly superior, to the older glues.

Interlocking joints are those which are cut in such a way that the pieces fit together like a puzzle. The interweaving of the parts, along with a glue bond, is enough to form strong joints for many purposes. Among these joints are box joints, splined joints, middle and end laps, tee laps, mortise and tenon, open tenon, milled dado box corner, dovetail dado, and lock joints, as illustrated in Figure 366.

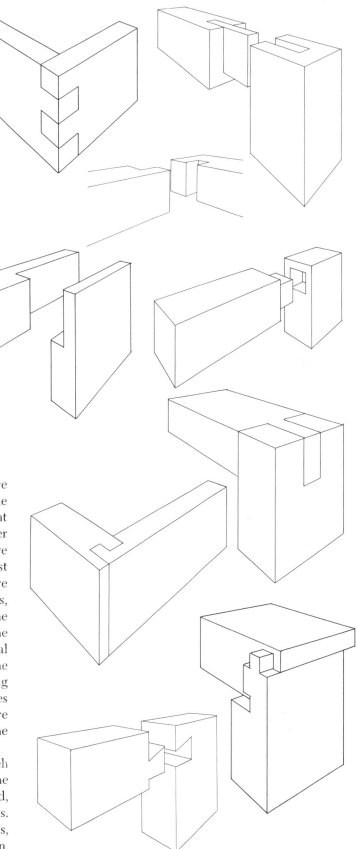

Figure 366.

METAL

Of the three ways of building up metals, the one most commonly used for sculpture is welding. Mechanical fastening with self-tapping screws, with nuts and bolts, and with rivets, and adhesive joining with glues or cement, have not been greatly exploited as sculptural joining systems.

Rivets have been used to join materials for almost as long as metal has been used by man. In their simplest form, they are shafts of metal with expanded ends, which prevent the fastened material from slipping off. Unlike the nut and bolt, a rivet alone will not pull pieces together, but also unlike the nut and bolt, solid rivets can be expanded by impact so that they swell (upset), filling their holes (preventing side movement) and gripping the joined materials firmly. Sound riveting requires that the hole drilled for the rivet be just large enough for a snug fit.

Usual practice requires that a heavy bar of iron (bucking bar) be placed against the head of the rivet while the shank of the rivet is swollen by impact from a ball peen hammer (Figure 373B) or a pneumatic riveting tool. Light blows will swell only the end of the shank, while heavy blows will cause the shank to swell along its full length.

A riveting tool is used to spread hollow rivets (Figure 372B). The flared head of the tool is centered over the opening in the shank of the hollow rivet (Figure 367), and struck — squarely and repeatedly — until the wedging action of the tool forces the walls of the rivet to spread. Washers are sometimes used on rivets to prevent them from pulling through soft materials.

A tool known as a "pop riveter," which has been used in industry for many years and is now available in an inexpensive household model, allows riveting in blind spots (where the head of the rivet is not accessible). A rivet is placed in the tool (Figure 368), and the shank of the rivet is placed through the holes in the material to be joined (Figure 369). If necessary, a washer can be placed over the shank of the rivet (Figure 370) before the handle of the rivet tool is depressed. When the handle is squeezed, the tool pulls the long shaft through the hollow rivet, drawing behind it a large knob, which swells the rivet. When the head of the shaft wedges itself tightly inside the rivet (against the riveted material), the shaft breaks free (Figure 371) at a weak point on the shaft immediately behind the head.

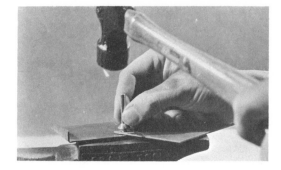

Figure 367.

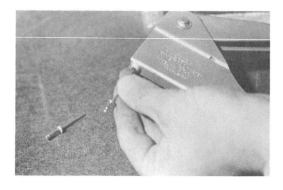

Figure 368.

Figure 369.

Figure 370.

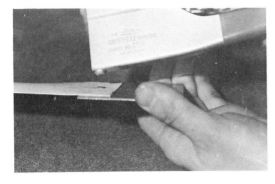

Figure 371.

Rivet Types and Tools

a. Brazier head split rivets — for soft materials (Figure 372A)

b. Rivet tool for hollow rivets (Figure 372B)

c. Flat head hollow rivets (Figure 372C)

d. Brazier head hollow rivets (Figure 372D)

e. Brazier head solid iron rivets (Figure 372E)

f. Countersunk solid rivets and burrs (washers) (Figure 372F)

g. Aircraft-grade aluminum brazier rivets (note the identification mark on the head) (Figure 372G)

h. Brazier head soft aluminum rivets (Figure 372H)

i. Pop rivets and washers (Figure 372I)

j. Bucking bar (Figure 373A)

k. Ball peen hammer (Figure 373B)

Figure 372.

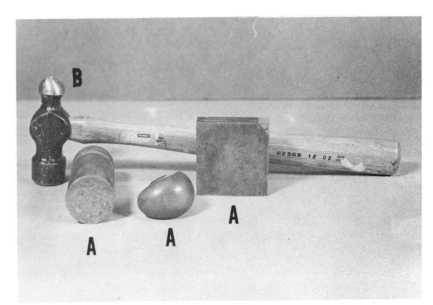

Figure 373.

Figure 374. Welded metal figures, N. Coleman.

Figure 375. *Two Faces of Eve,* David L. Cayton, American (1940-   ), welded metal.

Figure 376. *Wife of Dedaelus,* David L. Cayton, American (1940-   ), welded metal.

Welding

Welding is the process of joining similar metals by melting both metals along a common joint line and causing the molten metal to flow together, forming one unit. A filler of a similar metal is often used to build up thickness or strength along the joint line, or anywhere else that thickness is needed. Brazing is similar to welding, in that the intent is to join metals through application of heat, but the metals need not be similar, and they are not melted. Instead, a foreign metal, with a low melting joint, is melted between the metals to be joined, and on cooling, the foreign metal acts like a glue, bonding to both metals. A brazed joint does not have the strength of a welded joint and should not be used for joints which will be stressed or flexed.

Cutting

Cutting is the action of burning away a thin channel (kerf) of ferrous metal, in order to separate the metal into more than one piece or shape. Nonferrous metals will not oxidize rapidly enough to be cut with a cutting torch; instead, these metals can be separated by melting a section of metal, blasting the molten metal away with a sharp blast of oxygen from the cutting torch (page 118), and then continuing this action until a kerf is formed.

Electric Spot Welding

Electric spot welding, as a system of joining metal, is of limited but valuable use to the sculptor. The primary use of the spot welder is to join like ferrous metals at particular points, or along a continuous path of points. The technique does not offer the potential of modifying surfaces, of joining unlikes (rods to the center of flat sheets), or of building across open spaces (as is possible with gas welding), but warping from excessive heat and scar-like beads (both common to gas welding) are almost completely eliminated. In addition to these advantages, no skill is required to operate most spot welders (Figure 377); they are almost completely automatic. The metal to be welded is placed between the jaws of the welder (Figure 378), and the machine is then activated, in this case by depressing the handle. A proper weld (Figure 379) will be small and circular, about the size and shape of the jaws, and will be stronger than the surrounding metal.

Gas Welding

Gas welding, a method of creating heat for a weld by burning gas, primarily oxygen and acetylene, is used by the artist in ways which would be considered strange and unprofessional, if not unsafe, by the mechanic or technician. Frequently, the artist uses the torch to build masses of metal, layers thick, only to

Figure 377.

Figure 378.

Figure 379.

cut into the layers with a cutting torch, or to braze a thin layer of brass over the surface of sheet iron, for the sole purpose of creating color or texture (at the expense of the strength of the iron sheet). The artist is not always concerned with achieving strength in his welding, so it is permissible for him to deliberately burn crusts of scale on the surface of the metal, if that particular visual effect is desired, even though burning the metal in this way might weaken the structure of the metal.

The primary seams used by the artist for gas welding are the overlapping weld (Figure 380B), the butt weld (Figure 380A), and the flange weld (Figure 380C). Only similar metals may be welded with these seams. The technique of welding either seam is similar, except for the positioning of the metal during the weld (page 116).

Tools Required

a. Acetylene cylinder (Figure 381F). The acetylene cylinder is a low pressure tank. The acetylene gas is absorbed by sponge-like liquid acetone, which keeps the gas stable and allows the pressure to remain low. Three hundred cubic feet of the gas can be dissolved at 250 p/si at 70° F. The pressure reading on the acetylene pressure gauge is not an accurate indicator of the total volume of gas remaining in the cylinder. To determine the contents of the cylinder, it must be weighed. Each pound over empty weight is equal to 14½ cu. ft. of gas. Acetylene is *dangerous*, as it is explosive and anesthetic, but its presence can be easily detected by its odor.

Figure 380.

Figure 381.

b. Oxygen cylinder (Figure 382F). Oxygen is bottled in high pressure tanks and is usually obtained charged from 1,800 – 3,000 p/si of pressure. The oxygen cylinder pressure gauge will accurately indicate the contents of the tank. The gas is not normally harmful, but large quantities of pure oxygen should not be breathed. Oxygen does not burn, but it can cause some materials, like grease or oil, to burst into flame or explode; therefore, *do not get grease or oil on the tanks, torches,* *valves, or gauges.* Oxygen tanks can also explode if subjected to shock or excessive heat. Never use gas tanks unless they are fastened firmly in an upright position.

c. Torch (Figure 383). The torch consists of a welding tip (Figure 383A), mixing handle (Figure 383B), and gas valves (Figures 383C, and 383D). The cutting torch consists of the cutting tip (Figure 384A), cutting attachment (Figure 384B), mixing handle (Figure 384C), cutting oxygen

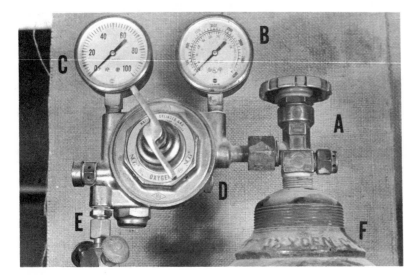

Figure 382.

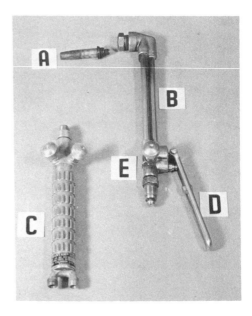

Figure 384.

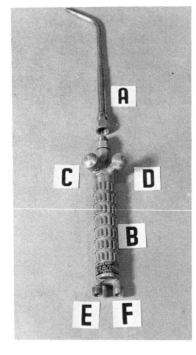

Figure 383.

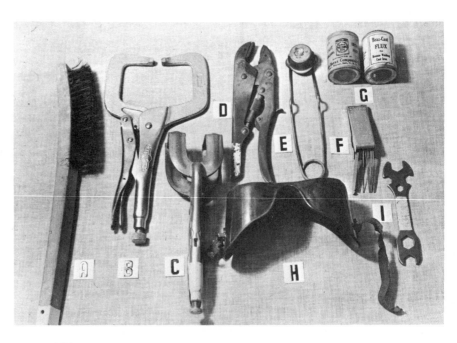

Figure 385.

valve (Figure 384D), and the oxygen valve (Figure 384E).

d. Oxygen and acetylene regulators (Figures 382 and 381). Each regulator consists of two pressure gauges and a pressure valve (Figures 381B, 381C, 381D, 382B, 382C, 382D). There are two hoses, one for each regulator. The green hose carries oxygen and the red carries the acetylene.

e. Flint or spark lighter (Figure 385E)

f. Dark goggles (Figure 385H)

g. Wrenches (Figure 385I)

h. Gloves

i. Tongs (Figure 133A)

j. Wire brush (Figure 385A)

k. Tip cleaners (Figure 385F)

l. Pliers (Figures 385B, 385C, and 385D)

m. Fluxes (Figure 385G)

n. Power grinder

Installation of Regulators on Tanks

1. Open the tank valve momentarily to clean the valve seat (Figures 381A and 382A).

2. Turn the regulator valves off (counterclockwise) (Figures 381D and 382D).

3. Attach the regulator to the proper tank. The oxygen tank has a right-hand (clockwise) female thread; The acetylene tank has a left-hand (counterclockwise) male thread.

4. Attach the green hose to the oxygen outlet on the oxygen regulator (right-hand thread) (Figure 382E).

5. Attach the red hose to the acetylene outlet on the acetylene regulator (left-hand thread) (Figure 381E).

6. Blow gas through the hoses by opening the tank valves (Figures 381A and 382A), and momentarily opening the regulator valves (Figures 381D and 382D). Close the tank valves, then shut off the regulator valve.

7. Attach the hoses to the proper inlets on the mixing handle (Figures 383E and 383F) of the torch. The oxygen inlet has a right-hand thread, the acetylene inlet a left-hand thread.

8. Install the welding tip (Figure 383A).

Operation

Each brand of welding equipment has its own operating requirements, so manufacturer's operating instructions should be consulted before the equipment is assembled or used. In general, equipment will be operated as indicated in the following paragraphs.

To Light the Torch

1. Select and install the proper tip for the thickness and kind of metal to be welded (Figure 383A).

2. Check the manufacturer's pressure chart for the proper pressures for the thickness and kind of metal to be welded.

3. Adjust the oxygen pressure:
   a. Open the oxygen tank valve all the way. (Figure 382A);
   b. Open the torch acetylene valve one-half turn (Figure 383D);
   c. Open the oxygen regulator valve until the proper reading appears on the delivery gauge (Figure 382C);
   d. Close the torch oxygen valve.

4. Adjust the acetylene pressure:
   a. Open the acetylene tank valve three quarters of a turn (Figure 381A);
   b. Open the torch acetylene vale one-half turn (Figure 383C);
   c. Open the acetylene regulator valve until the proper reading appears on the delivery gauge (Figure 381C);
   d. Close the torch acetylene valve.

5. Light the torch:
   a. Put on dark goggles;
   b. Open the torch acetylene valve one-half turn;
   c. Spark the lighter at the end of the welding tip to ignite the gas (Figure 386).
   d. Open the torch acetylene valve further, until the flame is strong enough that there is no soot floating away from the flame — the flame should remain in contact with the tip, however.
   e. Slowly open the torch oxygen valve until the proper flame is achieved (see Step 6).
   f. If the flame jumps away from the tip, either the pressure is too high at the regulator, the torch valves are open too far, or the welding tip is dirty and needs to be cleaned.

Figure 386.

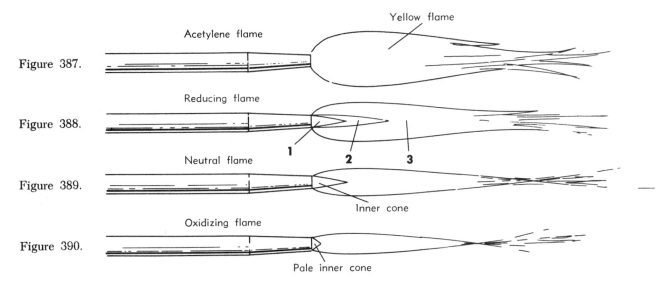

Figure 387.

Acetylene flame

Yellow flame

Figure 388.

Reducing flame

1   2   3

Figure 389.

Neutral flame

Inner cone

Figure 390.

Oxidizing flame

Pale inner cone

6. The flame. Four kinds of flame are possible with a welding torch.
   a. The acetylene flame is smoky yellow and of little use except for depositing a layer of soot (Figure 387).
   b. The reducing flame has too little oxygen and is used to avoid burning a crust on the molten metal. There are three distinct areas visible in the flame (Figure 388):
      (1) Brilliant white inner cone;
      (2) Glare-white "feather";
      (3) Violet or pale blue transparent outer cone.
   c. The neutral flame is the flame considered proper for most welding. Oxygen is added to the flame until the glare-white feather of the reducing flame just disappears (Figure 389).
   d. The oxidizing flame contains an excess of oxygen. The glare-white feather disappears, and the inner cone becomes pale. This flame will burn scale into the molten metal (Figure 390).
7. Turn off the torch:
   a. Turn off the torch acetylene valve;
   b. Turn off the torch oxygen valve.
8. Drain the gauges before putting the equipment away. Do not leave gas in the lines for extended periods of time.
   a. Close both cylinder valves;
   b. Open the torch oxygen valve to drain the oxygen hose, regulator, and gauge. The indicated pressure at the gauges should drop to zero;
   c. Close the oxygen regulator valve, and remove the key;
   d. Close the torch oxygen valve;

e. Open the torch acetylene valve, and drain the lines, gauges, and regulator. The indicated pressure on both gauges should drop to zero;
f. Close the acetylene regulator valve, and remove the key;
g. Close the acetylene torch valve.

If the pressure gauge on either bank begins to climb, that tank valve is not closed tight, and the valve should be tightened and the draining process repeated for that particular tank, to prevent damage to the regulator and to eliminate a potential safety hazard.

Welding a Seam

1. Clean the areas to be welded.
2. Place and clamp the metal, if necessary, into position. For a butt weld, join the sheets along their edges, but do not place them tightly together to start the weld. Leave a 1/16″ gap at the start of the weld and a 3/16″ gap for each foot at the end of the weld, in order to prevent buckling. Overlapping seams simply have the sheets overlapping between 5 and 10 times the thickness of an individual sheet.
3. Light the torch (page 115).
4. Tack weld the corners by heating the metal at the start of the weld until the metal of the pieces flow together. The torch should be held with the white cone about 1/16″ from the metal, at a 30° angle pointing towards the weld line, and moved in a small horizontal or vertical circle, depending on the thickness of the metal. The circular motion will aid the flow of the metal.
5. Start the weld by heating the seam at the flame end of the seam (Figure 391), until a puddle of molten metal is formed, then add welding rod to

Figure 391.

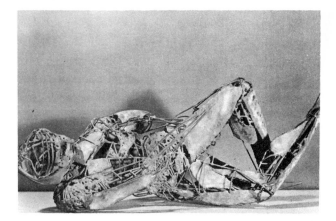

Figure 393.

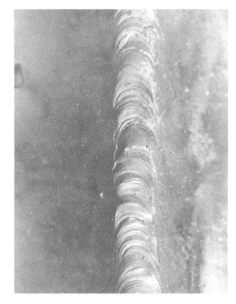

Figure 392.

Figure 394.

the puddle to be melted to act as a filler. Melt the rod with the puddle, not with the torch. The weld should progress in the direction of the flame, like a continuous tack weld (Step 4), with the addition of the welding rod as a filler (Figure 392). Thin metal should be welded with a vertical circular motion of the torch, to prevent burning holes in the seam; thick metals should be welded with a horizontal circle, so that both sides of the weld get enough heat to melt the metal.

Some metals, unlike soft iron, require special handling. Stainless steel should be welded with an acetylene feather about 1/16″ larger than the inner cone (reduction flame). The flame should be held at an 80° angle, with the tip of the inner cone 1/16″ from the work. Stir the puddle as little as possible. Cast iron welding should not be attempted by an

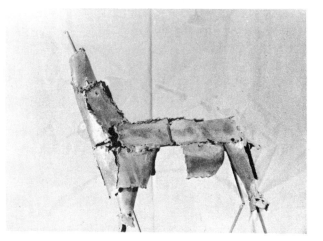

Figure 395.

Figure 396.

amateur welder; it requires special fluxes, slow move-ment, and preheating, to prevent damage to the cast. Aluminum is a difficult metal to weld unless a heliarc is utilized. Some aluminum alloys can be welded with an acetylene torch if special aluminum welding rod and aluminum flux are used, and if the torch is ad-justed for stainless steel. The metal should be pre-heated over a charcoal fire or a low gas flame until it is hot enough to cause a pine stick to smoulder when the stick is rubbed over the metal. The pieces to be welded must not touch each other or the puddle will collapse. The puddle must be kept small by flicking the flame up off of the puddle when necessary. Avoid the fumes of this weld.

Brazing
1. Clean the surfaces to be brazed.
2. Position and clamp the work.
3. Paint brazing flux on the metal, or heat the braz-ing rod with the torch and dip it into powdered flux.
4. Heat the metal to a dull red heat and apply the rod. The rod will melt and flow into the area of great-est heat. Capillary action will draw the brazing metal along the joint if the area of heat is moved ahead of the metal.

   Sheet iron can be coated (tinned or bronzed) for decorative or protective purposes, by cleaning the en-tire sheet, fluxing the area, and then brazing over the surface. Brazing rod can be obtained in various colors, including red, yellow, and even white, as in the case of nickel rod.

Cutting
Metals other than soft iron are difficult to cut. Stainless steel can be cut by laying mild steel rod into the kerf to dilute the chrome and nickel alloy. Cast iron should be avoided because it requires excessive amounts of oxygen and special cutting tips. Non-fer-rous metals, like copper and brass, can be separated by running a line of a paste made of iron cement (used in the repair of iron furnaces) and water, 1" wide along each side of the desired cut line. The metal is then heated with a torch until it is fluid, and the molten metal blown away with a blast of oxygen from the torch.

TO ADJUST THE TORCH FOR CUTTING
1. Refer to the manufacturer's pressure chart for proper tip and tank delivery pressure for the kind of metal and the thickness to be cut. Adjust the delivery regulator to deliver the proper pressure (page 115).
2. Remove the welding attachment from the mixing handle, if there is one, and attach the cutting at-tachment to the mixing handle (Figure 384B). Attach the cutting tip (Figure 384A). The cutting tip has at least five holes in the end (Figure 397A), unlike the welding tip, which has only one hole (Figure 397B).
3. If the cutting attachment has an oxygen adjust-ment valve, open the torch oxygen valve all of the way, and make the necessary oxygen adjust-ments with the cutting attachment oxygen valve (Figure 384E).
4. The cutting torch is lighted in the same way as the welding torch (page 115), except that the final adjustment is made with the oxygen cutting valve (Figure 384D) held open.

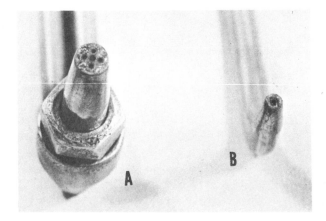

Figure 397.

TO CUT

1. Light the cutting torch.
2. Start heating the metal to be cut, on a line of cut, at the edge of the metal, if possible.
3. When the metal is cherry red, slowly press the oxygen cutting valve all the way open (Figure 398).
4. As the metal burns away, slowly move the flame along the line of cut so that new metal is continually being preheated for cutting. If the kerf closes behind the flame, the cutting action is too

Figure 400.

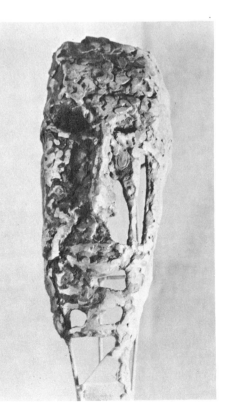

Figure 398.

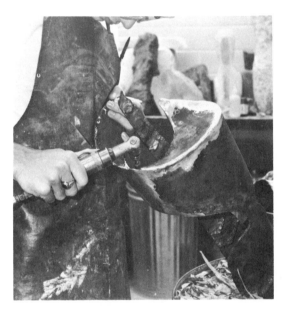

Figure 401.

Figure 399.

slow, or the tip is too far from the metal. If the cut is not all the way through the metal, or if the melting action stops, the motion is too fast, or the flame needs to be angled ahead in order to preheat the metal at a faster rate.

FINISHING WELDED METAL

Welded medal has a tendency to become texturally monotonous if left in its raw state. This bubbled, scale-like condition can be ground away, leaving a clean seam. If the weld disturbs an otherwise clean surface, all outward signs of the weld can be ground away.

Raw weld is susceptible to rapid rusting; so unless rust color and, eventually, total disintegration are acceptable, the metal must be protected. Over brazing, painting, clear lacquer coating, clear plastic coating, or oil coating are coverings utilized to prevent rusting. If warrented by the situation, the sculptures can be plated with a more resistant metal, such as copper, chrome, or nickel, for protective purposes.

WAX

Built-up wax sculpture is by nature rather fragile, not the least resistant to shock, heat, or abrasion, and so it is almost always coupled with the substitutive technique, the final result being a casting in metal (page 79). Sheets of wax (page 42) are cut with simple tools, such as a butter knife or mat knife, into the desired shapes and patterns. These wax sheets can be stretched, bent, and otherwise formed, and have their surfaces manipulated by warming the shapes or patterns before they are joined (Figures 402, 403, and 260). Joining can be effected either by pressing the edges of the shapes together with some force or by heating the wax along the seams until the joints melt and flow together. If the wax is not strong enough to support itself, a wire or pipe armature can be used for added strength.

Wax sculpture can also be built up of lumps of wax in much the same way that clay can be built up. Warm lumps of wax are pressed onto a wax core, building the desired form "from the inside out."

PLASTIC

Many plastic materials such as compounds and mixtures of polyesters, epoxies, acetates, PVC, polycarbonate, vinal, TFE fluorocarbons, acrylics, polypropylene, and phenolic are available for sculptural use. Most of these materials are similar in appearance, though each has individual characteristics. TFE fluorocarbon is probably the slipperiest of the plastics and, for all practical purposes, cannot be cemented. Epoxy resins are among the most adhesive of all materials; PVCs can be produced in an unlimited color range; and some acrylics can be heated from a rigid state to a rubbery one. Regardless of their similar characteristics, joining characteristics differ greatly. All can be bolted or riveted (page 110) except the fluid resins; some, like PVC, can be welded with hot air or hot helium; and some, like the acrylics, can be cemented.

Because plastics are found in both the rigid and fluid state, two additive systems are employed in their use. Mechanical and chemical joining are used for solid plastics; fluid or putty-like build-ups are used for the liquid plastics.

Figure 402.

Figure 403.

Solid Plastic

Acrylic plastic (plexiglass) is a thermoplastic material which can be softened with heat and will retain its shape when cooled. It is affected by some solutions such as gasoline, alcohol, benzene, carbon tetrachloride, acetone, de-icing fluid, and glass window cleaners — to the extent that they will craze, yellow, crack, and perhaps cause the plastic to become brittle.

Forming

Plexiglass can be formed by hand pressure if the sheets are heated from 290° F. to 340° F., in an oven or with heat lamps. Allow one minute of heat time for each 100th of an inch of thickness. Thin sheets should be heated a little higher than thick sheets because of the rapid heat loss in thin sheet stock. The operator should wear soft cotton gloves to prevent marring the stock. The formed sheet should be cooled slowly and evenly, while being held in its formed position.

Cutting

Plexiglass up to 1/8″ thick can be broken like glass, by scribing a line where the cut is desired, then bending the sheet over the edge of a table with the scribed line face up directly over the table edge. The sheet can also be cut with a band saw, circular saw, or jigsaw. Circular saw blades, 8″ — 10″ in diameter or larger, should turn at 3400 rpm, with 6 — 8 teeth per inch, alternately set and filed radially. The blades should be hollow-ground for thin sheets, and should not be raised higher than necessary, to prevent chipping. Sheet metal equipment should not be used to punch or shear acrylic plastic.

Drilling

Plexiglass can be drilled with a hot wire or twist drills. (Twist drills to be used for drilling plastic should be repointed as they are for drilling bronze.) The cutting edge should be ground to O° rake angle. The point included angle should be 55° to 60° where the sheet thickness is one hole diameter or less. The point angle should be increased for holes where the diameter is less than the sheet thickness. Moderate speed and light pressure should be used. Do not attempt to drill cold plexiglass; it should first be warmed to at least 70° F.

Machining

Tools used for machining plexiglass should be sharpened so that they have no rake — they should scrape not cut. If necessary, soapy water or kerosene can be used as a lubricant to prevent overheating of the part of the plastic being machined. In general, pressure on the tool should be light, and tool chatter avoided. Do not work cold plexiglass.

Cementing

Various plexiglass types require different cements. Some cements are solvents, and soften plastic (such as Plexiglas IIVVA) so that the softened surfaces can be pressed together to form a bond. Other cements are used as a glue on highly insoluble plexiglass (Plexiglas 55); in these cases, the cement simply bonds to each surface. Critical cement joints may require annealing to prevent crazing. To anneal plexiglass for cementing, first heat the plastic to 160° F. for 24 hours, or 175° F. for 10 hours, and then cool slowly. Cement the joint, and repeat the heating and cooling process.

Buffing

Plexiglass can be buffed to a high luster or transparency by lightly pressing the work against cotton rubbing wheels that are well lubricated with mutton tallow. The wheels should run at a speed of about 1300 — 1800 feet per minute — revolutions-per-minute depending on the diameter of the wheel. Commercial buffing compounds can be used if available. Do not permit the bluff to run against the plastic in one spot, or the plastic will melt and flow, or "burn."

Sanding

Plexiglass can be sanded with Wet or Dry sandpaper, grade 320 or finer. The paper should be wrapped around a flexible sanding block and lubricated with soapy water or kerosene. For control, the sanding block should be used in a circular motion with light pressure. Progressively finer paper should be used (360A, 400A, 500A, and finally 600A) for each sanding. The final luster or polish can be completed by buffing.

Fluid Plastic

Many plastics can be obtained in a fluid state so that they can be used to build up mass in the same way that cement or plaster is used to build up mass. Plastics, such as polyester and epoxy resins, which require the addition of a hardening agent, can be mixed with aggregates or fillers, to give color, to add to the bulk (significantly reducing cost), to produce desired textures, and most importantly, to greatly increase strength or machinability. Many of these resins are compounded with fillers and sold commercially as "liquid metal" to be used for patching auto bodies, leaking tanks, cement floors, and so on. Filler materials include glass fibers, talc, cement, dry pigment, silica flour (flint), dyes, stone chips, stone powder, metal chips or powder, wood flour, shell flour (walnut shells), cotton flock, sisal fiber, chopped paper, crepe paper, wood bark, soybean meal, ground feathers, asbestos, mica, clay, chalk, perlite, cork, and water soluble materials which can be dissolved from the plastic after it has hardened. It is necessary to formulate the matrix in such a way that the medium is putty-like (sag-resistant), but still fluid enough to retain its strength and adhesive ability.

Plastics which depend on evaporation to effect hardening, like some latexes and polyvinyl latexes, cannot be readily mixed with fillers by the sculptor because of their rapid hardening time. Some of these plastics are factory-mixed with fillers and sold commercially as self-hardening modeling compounds, plastic metal, or sealing compounds.

Polyesters and Epoxies

1. Construct an armature which occupies the bulk of the sculpture. If the armature can be designed in clay or wax, like a core, the core can be removed from the finished sculpture, leaving a hollow shell, and reducing the weight of the sculpture considerably.

2. Dry mix the filler material to an even consistency. Enough aggregate should be premixed to complete the entire sculpture.

3. Mix a small quantity of the aggregate, resin, and hardening agent. It is important that the manufacturer's directions are followed, as each resin requires a different hardening agent, in various amounts — depending on hardening time, curing time, and temperature. Only enough plastic should be mixed as can be used within its hardening time.

4. If raw resin is used, mix the resin with its appropriate hardening agent. In most cases, raw resin must be reinforced with some material like fiberglass mat.

5. Apply the resin with wood or metal spatulas, in the case of aggregates, and with brush or roller for raw resins.

6. Many aggregates cure with an unpleasant glossy surface, which will hide the texture and color of the aggregate. This gloss can be removed by sanding or light grinding.

7. The surface of the plastic can be modified by filing, grinding, and cutting, but chiseling should be avoided because aggregates may cause brittleness or otherwise be unpredictable, when subjected to heavy impact from sharp tools.

Polyvinyl Latex

1. Construct a rigid armature which will also serve as a core, and which will have a coarse texture, such as window screen or plaster lath. If the sculpture is to be bulky, form the core to within 1/8″ or 1/4″ of the finished surface, in order to reduce the amount of material needed, and to reduce weight.

2. Remove a small quantity of the putty-like material from the container (enough for about 15 minutes' work) and apply the plastic in thin layers, with metal or wood tools. Thick applications tend to become crumbly. Areas requiring thick sections should be built up slowly in thin layers, allowing adequate time between applications for thorough hardening.

3. The surface of this material can be modified by filing, grinding, drilling, cutting, and sanding, if excess heat is avoided.

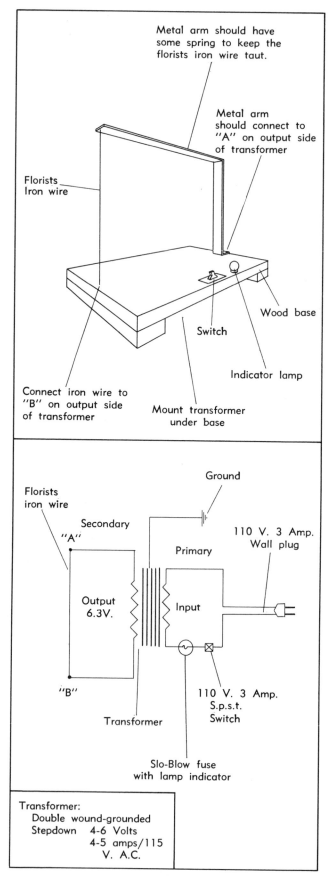

Figure 404.

APPENDIX

Weights and Measures

Volume and Liquid Equivalents

4 gills = 1 pint
2 pints = 1 quart
4 quarts = 1 gallon
1 gallon = 231 cubic inches

Fluid Measure

Gallons	Pints	Ounces	Drachms
1	8	128	1,024
	1	16	128
		1	8

1 pint (16 ounces) = 1 fluid pound

Troy Weight (for Weighing Precious Metals)

Pounds	Ounces	Pennyweights	Grains	Grams
1	12	240	5,760	373.24
	1	20	480	31.10
		1	24	1.56

Avoirdupois Weight (for Weighing Chemicals)

Pounds	Ounces	Drachms	Grains (Troy)	Grams
1	16	256	7,000	453.60
	1	16	437.5	28.35
		1	27.34	1.77

Fahrenheit (F.) = 9/5 centigrade (C.) +32
Centigrade (C.) = 5/9 fahrenheit (F.) −32

Weights of Materials by Cubic Inch

Brass	.2960 lb.	Zinc (cast)	.248 lb.
Aluminum	.0924 lb.	Fir	.0199 lb.
Copper	.3184 lb.	Lignum Vitae	.0397 lb.
Steel	.2816 lb.	Mahogany	.0325 lb.
Cast iron	.2599 lb.	Fired red clay	.065 lb.
Bronze	.3194 lb.	Portland cement	.1119 lb.
Lead	.407 lb.	Marble	.0975 lb.
Silver	.38 lb.	Plaster of Paris	.065 lb.
Gold	.697 lb.	Sandstone	.083 lb.

Volume

To find the volume of a sphere, multiply the cube of the diameter by 0.5236.

To find the volume of a cylinder, multiply the circumference by 1/4 the diameter, then multiply the product so obtained by the length of the cylinder.

To find the volume of a cube, multiply the length by the width by the height.

1 U.S. gal. = 1.3368 cu. ft.
1 cu. ft. = 7.481 U.S. gal.
1 gal. water (62° F.) = 8.336 lbs.
1 lb. water (62° F.) = .1199 gal.

COMMON RECIPES

(Unless otherwise indicated, proportions are given in volumes.)

Slip Clay for Slip Casting

Kentucky ball clay #4	16	parts by weight
Kentucky ball clay	16	parts by weight
Kentucky ball clay special	2	parts by weight
Plastic vitrox	16	parts by weight
Talc	50	parts by weight
Whiting	3	parts by weight
Water	50.5	parts by weight
Silicate of soda	0.4	parts by weight
Soda ash	0.1	parts by weight

Slip Clay for Slip Casting

Red art clay*	66.3	parts by weight
Water	33.7	parts by weight
Soda ash	0.14	parts by weight
Sodium silicate ("N" Brand)	0.4	parts by weight

Mix the electrolyte with the water before sifting in the clay.

*Cedar Heights Clay Co.

Slip Clay for Slip Casting

Kentucky ball clay #4	38	parts by weight
Kentucky ball clay special	38	parts by weight
China clay	25	parts by weight
Plastic vitrox	224	parts by weight
Talc	1.75	parts by weight
Water	232	parts by weight
Sodium silicate	1.6	parts by weight
Soda ash	0.75	parts by weight

Low-Melting Alloys for Casting in Metal

Lipowitz's alloy — soften at 140° F., melts at 158° F.; silver-white.

Cadmium	3 parts
Tin	4 parts
Bismuth	15 parts
Lead	8 parts

Cadmium alloy with a melting point of 179.5° F.

Cadmium	2 parts
Tin	3 parts
Bismuth	16 parts
Lead	11 parts

Cadmium alloy with a melting point of 167° F.

Cadmium	10 parts
Tin	3 parts
Lead	8 parts
Bismuth	8 parts

Wood's metal — melts between 140° F. and 161.5° F.; platinum color

Lead	4 parts
Tin	2 parts
Bismuth	5-8 parts
Cadmium	1-2 parts

Alloy for reproducing woodcuts or medallions

Tin	3 parts
Lead	13 parts
Bismuth	6 parts

Alloy for reproducing woodcuts or medallions

Tin	6 parts
Lead	8 parts
Bismuth	14 parts

Wax to be poured for a cast

Paraffin	8	parts by weight
Carnauba wax	1	parts by weight
Rosin	2	parts by weight

Wax to be poured for a cast

White beeswax	4	parts by weight
Paraffin	3.5	parts by weight
Talc	2.5	parts by weight
Cornstarch	2	parts by weight

Wax to be brushed on to form a cast

Paraffin	12	parts by weight
Rosin	14	parts by weight
Carnauba wax	2	parts by weight
Talc	3	parts by weight
Zinc oxide	0.5	parts by weight

Wax for making molds

Paraffin	54	parts by weight
Bayberry wax	21	parts by weight
Carnauba wax	5	parts by weight
Stearic acid	20	parts by weight

Wax for making molds

Beeswax, yellow	1 pound
Linseed oil	½ pint
Tallow	1 pound
Flour or talc	2 pounds

Wax for making molds

Mix paraffin, olive oil, and whiting or talc to desired quality. Use talc to separate the model from the wax.

Wax for modeling

Mobile wax 2300 may be softened with Vaseline or stiffened with paraffin.

Wax for modeling

Microcrystalline 3602 wax — add Venice turpentine or Vaseline to condition the wax for winter or summer.

Wax for modeling

Yellow beeswax	4 parts by weight
Venice turpentine	1 parts by weight

Wax for modeling

Esso Microvan 1650, and motor oil to soften to suit.

Wax for modeling

Dental wax, soften with Venice turpentine and harden with paraffin.

Wax for modeling

Candle wax, white	8	parts by weight
Venice turpentine	1.5	parts by weight
Flake white	1	parts by weight

Wax for modeling

Burgundy pitch	1	parts by weight
Beeswax	10	parts by weight
Tallow	1	parts by weight
Venice turpentine	1	parts by weight

Wax for modeling

Paraffin	14	parts by weight
Beeswax	16	parts by weight
Lanolin	1	parts by weight
Venice turpentine	1	parts by weight
Lead oleate	1	parts by weight

Wax for modeling

Beeswax, white	10	parts by weight
Paraffin	10	parts by weight
Vaseline	5	parts by weight
Cocoa butter	2.5	parts by weight
Lanolin (to harden) up to 1		parts by weight
Druggists' lead*	5	parts by weight

*Prepare druggists' lead by boiling together, in water, equal parts of lead monoxide, olive oil, and lard.

NOTE

Waxes should be melted in a double boiler, not directly over an open flame. Do not spill water into the molten wax, or a violent eruption of hot fluid wax may result. To make thin sheets of wax, pour the molten wax onto sheets of wet plywood or formica. If the wax tends to stick, either the plywood was not wet enough, or the wax was too hot.

Pitch for repoussé

Burgundy pitch	8 parts by weight
Tallow, mustard oil, or linseed oil	1 parts by weight
Pumice, plaster, or brick dust	add to the density desired

Pitch for repoussé

Burgundy pitch	10.	parts by weight
Tallow	0.5	parts by weight
Plaster or talc	4.	parts by weight

Separators for casting and molding

To Separate (Mold)	From (Cast)	Treat the Mold
Rubber	Plaster	Rinse with soapy water.
Rubber	Wax	Rinse with soapy water.
Metal	Plaster	Lard or fish oil.
Plaster	Plaster	A solution of gum mastic and amyl alcohol; or a solution of yellow beeswax and carbon tetrachloride; or a solution of hot water, 10 parts; shellac powder, 1 part; and borax, ½ part; or English crown soap (potters mold soap); or solution of one cake of Ivory soap, chipped into a gallon of water. Simmer for an hour and add 4 drops of kerosene.
Plaster	Wax	Soapy water.
Wood	Cement	Paraffin dissolved in coal oil.

Iron	Cement	Coal oil or 3-in-1 oil.
Plaster	Cement	Mutton tallow and coal oil mixture.
Glue	Cement	Coat with 3-in-1 oil.

Investments for nonferrous metals

a. Nonferrous investment #1 (U.S. Gypsum)

b.
Number 1 molding plaster, white	1 part
Luto	1 part
Water	as required

c.
Number 1 molding plaster	2 parts
Silica flour (flint)	2 parts
Luto	3 parts
Water	as required

d. PVI #10

Water — as directed by manufacturer

Investment for aluminum only

a.
Number 1 molding plaster	5	parts by weight
Sawdust	1	parts by weight
Sand	28	parts by weight
Water	16	parts by weight

(Allow to cure overnight, then heat at 190° F. for 2-4 hours, then heat to 575° F. for 1-2 hours.)

b.
Number 1 molding plaster	1 part
Pumice	1 part
Water	as required

Investment core for nonferrous metal

Plaster	1 part
Silica flour (flint)	1 part
Asbestos fiber	1 part
Water	as required

Investment for lead casting

a.
Plaster of Paris	10 parts by weight
Asbestos fibers	12 parts by weight
Chalk	4 parts by weight
Marble dust	4 parts by weight

(Dry and warm the investment before casting.)

b.
Plaster # 1 molding	6 parts by weight
Chalk	3 parts by weight
Crushed grog	3 parts by weight
Marble dust	3 parts by weight

Sulphur molds for metal masters or dies

Flowers of sulphur	8 parts
Iron filings (cleaned of oil)	1 part

(Melt together and pour over the metal master; use grease as a separator.)

Core sand — for strong and intricate cores

Sharp sand	50 parts
Linseed oil (boiled)	1 parts

(Heat the cores to between 350° F. and 425° F.; never exceed 500° F.)

Core sand — for small cores

Beach sand	10 parts
Flour	1 parts

(Mix with molasses water; dry with heat.)

Core sand — for large cores

Sharp fire sand	8 parts
Strong loamy sand	2 parts
Flour	1.5 parts

(Mix with clay water; dry with gentle heat.)

(1) Core sand — for small, intricate cores

Beach sand	15 parts
Fire sand	15 parts
Rosin	2 parts
Flour	1 parts

(Mix with molasses water and dry with heat — too much water will make the sand stick; too little, crumble.)

(2) Core sand — for small, intricate cores

Beach sand	15 parts
Molding sand	5 parts
Flour	2 parts
Core oil	1 parts

(Mix with molasses water; dry with heat.)

Foundation cement for built-up cement

First application:	Portland cement	3 parts
	Lime putty (aged)	1 parts
	Hydrated lime	7% by weight
Second application:	Portland cement	2 parts
	Clean sand	1 parts
	Hydrated lime	5% by weight
Finish application:	Portland cement	4 parts
	Lime putty	1 parts
	Hydrated lime	add up to 10% to increase plasticity, if required

Stucco — for built-up cement

a.
Portland cement	1 parts
Lime	1 parts
Sand	6 parts

b.
Portland cement	1 parts
Lime	2 parts
Sand	5 parts

(Second mix more plastic than preceding mix.)

Common mortar

Portland cement	1 parts
Sand	3 parts

Cement accelerators

Calcium chloride (over 1%, but less than 3%), ammonium carbonate, alkalai carbonates (carbon dioxide), aluminum chloride, and magnesium chloride.

Cement retarders

Ferric chloride, if less than 2%, ammonium bicarbonate, ferrous bicarbonate, calcium sulphate, and plaster of Paris in small quantities. Sugar can completely retard the setting of cement. Aggregates in cement can be exposed by spraying a solution of sugar water over fresh cement. When the underlayer has hardened, the top soft skim of cement can be brushed away with a stiff brush.

Plaster accelerators

a. Heat the mix water.
b. Add 1 teaspoon of sodium chloride to each quart of mix water.
c. Add 1 teaspoon of potassium alum to each quart of mix water.
d. Add 1 part of a saturated solution of potassium sulphate and water to each 10 parts of mix water.
e. Add 10% lime.

Plaster retarders

a. Add 1 part saturated solution of borax and water to each 10 parts of mix water.
b. Add carpenter's glue to the mix water.
c. Add ½ teaspoon of calcined lime to each quart of mix water.
d. Add alcohol, sugar, or citric acid to the mix water.

Plaster — to harden the surface

a. Brush with lime water.
b. Brush with a hot saturated solution of potassium alum and water.
c. Immerse in boiling 2% solution of borax or in a saturated solution of sodium bicarbonate.

Plaster — to harden

a. Add magnesium fluosilicate to the mix water, from 4% to 5%.
b. Add 1 part white dextrine or gum arabic to 100 parts of plaster.
c. Add 5% white portland cement to the plaster.

Plaster — to seal for outdoor use

Mix the plaster with lime water. When dry, coat with hot boiled linseed oil at least three times. Paint with linseed oil varnish and cover with white oil paint. Every part of the plaster must be sealed, including the bottom.

Plaster — to seal with wax

Dry and warm the plaster, and coat with a solution of stearin and turpentine.

Plaster — to make soluble molds

Number 1 molding plaster	3 parts
Potato starch	1 part

Mix dry and add to water in the usual fashion. The finished mold can be dissolved away with boiling water. Do not pour the casting with the soluble mix.

Cement — to color

The following pigments should be mixed into the cement by machine, or an even color cannot be obtained:

Iron oxide, 5% to 10% — red, yellow, brown, black
Manganese dioxide, up to 10% — black, brown
Chromium oxide, 8% — green
Ultramarine blue, to 10% — blue
Carbon (plumbago, charcoal), to 10% — black
Red lead, 8% — red
Zinc white, to 20% — white
(Pigments utilizing artificial fillers such as talc should not be used.)

Plaster — to color

Polished white: Brush a thin solution of Ivory soap flakes onto the plaster, and polish with a soft cloth. Then make a thicker soap solution and repeat the first step until a satisfactory surface is obtained.

White opaque: Brush the plaster with white liquid shoe polish, then polish with a soft cloth.

Plaster — to color with a shellac vehicle

Mix 1 part clear shellac and 1 part alcohol to form a vehicle. Add dry pigment such as powdered tempera to the shellac, and rub the color into the plaster. Unwanted color can be removed with alcohol. To prevent streaking, brush a layer of shellac over the plaster before applying color.

Plaster — to color with an oil vehicle

Mix 1 part rectified turpentine and 1 part artist grade linseed oil to form a vehicle. Add dry pigment and brush or rub onto the plaster. To prevent streaking, paint the plaster with a coat of the vehicle before adding color. This vehicle is compatible with artists' oil colors, which can be used for the color instead of the dry pigment.

Cement (glue) — for stone

a. Yellow resin (or equal parts yellow
   resin and beeswax)   1 part
   Plaster of Paris   ½ part

Melt the ingredients together and apply to the heated stone. Allow to cool.

b. Gum arabic (thick solution) 1   part by weight
   #1 molding plaster   1.5   part by weight
   Quicklime   0.34 part by weight

Mix the ingredients and apply to the heated stone.

Wood — to bleach

a. Treat with sodium hypochlorite (clorox)

b. Apply oxalic acid (5% to 10%); flush with water, and dry; then apply sodium bisulphite (10%); flush with water, and dry.

Plastic wood (wood filler)

a. Wood flour   100 ounces
   Castor oil   ½ fluid ounce
   Acetone   ½ fluid ounce
   Rosin (powdered)   ½ ounce
   Alcohol   ½ fluid ounce

Mix the powders, mix the liquids, then mix the two. Keep in airtight container.

b. Wood glue (gelatin)   heat and boil
   Tissue paper   shred and add to
   Linseed oil   boiling glue
   Chalk

Mix to a paste, so that it will crumble when cold but will become pliable when warmed in the hand. This material can be pressed into molds and will dry in two or three days.

c. Xylol   1   quart
   Acetone   1¼   pint
   Ethyl acetate   1   pint
   Castor oil   6   drams
   Celluloid   1½   pounds (Avoirdupois)
   Wood flour   to suit

Mix the xylol, acetone, and ethyl acetate, then add the castor oil and celluloid, and allow to dissolve. Add the wood flour to the desired consistency.

Liquid or cold solder

Butyl acetate	1	part by weight
Ethyl acetate	7	part by weight
Methyl acetate	7	part by weight
Benzol	8	part by weight
Methyl alcohol	3	part by weight
Toluol	4.5	part by weight
Gum ester	0.75	part by weight
Proxyline	2	part by weight
Metal powder	4 to 5; add the kind and color to suit	

Mix all materials except metal powder in an airtight container by shaking. Mix in the metal powder when desired.

Oil base clay

Kaolin	56	parts
Sulphur	24	parts
Lithopone	20	parts

Dry mix these materials; add the following materials until the desired plasticity is attained.

Lanolin	60%
Glycerine	40%

Color may be added as desired (chrome oxide or burnt sienna).

Oil base clay

Ball clay
Lanolin
Glycerine

Mix to achieve the plasticity desired.

Soldering and tinning fluxes

a. Tin: Muriatic acid (saturate with zinc)   1   part
   Water   2   part
   Ammonium chloride   0.1 part

b. Brass and copper: Muriatic acid   1 pound
   Zinc   4 ounces
   Ammonium chloride   5 ounces

c. Iron: Muriatic acid   1 pound
   Tallow   6 ounces
   Ammonium chloride   4 ounces

d. Gold and silver: Muriatic acid   1 pound
   Tallow   8 ounces
   Ammonium chloride   8 ounces

Pickling solutions for brass, bronze, and copper

a. Potassium chloride   1 ounce
   Hydrochloric acid   5 ounces
   Water   40 fluid ounces

b. Ferric Chloride   2 ounces
   Water   3 ounces

c. Nitric acid   2 parts
   Sulphuric acid   1 part

d. Nitric acid   1 quart

d.	Nitric acid	1 quart
	Sulphuric acid	1 quart
	Muriatic acid	1 gill
	Water	1 pint
e.	Matt dip:	
	Hydroflouric acid	2 pints
	Nitric acid	1 pint
	Muriatic acid	½ pint
	Water	5 pints

Store in a wax lined container.

f.	Matt dip:	
	Hydrochloric acid	1 part
	Sulphuric acid	6 parts
	Water	6 parts

Copper, brass, and bronze cleaner

a. Apply a solution of 6% acetic acid, saturated with table salt, to the metal with a wool cloth.

b. Rub the metal with oxalic acid, then polish with a paste of 1 part oxalic acid and 4 parts tripoli.

Cast iron pickle

Vitriol	1 part
Water	2 parts

Apply with an acid-proof brush, rinse with water after 10 hours. Brush away scale.

Pickle for iron and steel

a.	Hydrochloric acid	2 parts
	Water	1 part
b.	Sulphuric acid	1 part
	Water	100 parts

Pickle for Aluminum

a. Immerse in boiling potassium hydroxide, then plunge into nitric acid, rinse and dry (for pure aluminum only).

b. Mat dip: plunge into hot bath of 10% sodium hydroxide solution, saturated with table salt; wash; brush; and repeat. Dry in sawdust.

Aluminum — to Decolorize

Wash with a mixture of 30 parts borax, 1000 parts water, 1/2 teaspoon ammonia.

Lead — to Clean

Immerse in a 6%, or stronger, solution of acetic acid.

Iron and Steel — to Color

a. To blue iron or steel:
Dissolve 14 parts sodium hyposulphate in 100 parts of water.
Dissolve 3.5 parts lead acetate in 100 parts of water.
Mix the two solutions, boil, and immerse the metal to be blued.

b. Clean the metal with potassium bichromate/sulphuric acid mixture.
Wash with ammonium hydroxide and dry.
Apply ammonium polysulphide to obtain the desired color.
Dry and rub with soft cloth to polish.
Repeat the application if necessary.
Polish with boiled linseed oil.

c. Blue-black on iron or steel:
Immerse the metal in a hot solution of sodium thiosulphate and water.

d. Blue-black:

Nitric acid	15 parts
Coppersulphate	8 parts
Alcohol	20 parts
Water	125 parts

Spread over dry, clean metal. Dry and rub with soft cloth.

e. Blue-black:
Prepare a solution of tin chloride, 1 part; hydrochloric acid, 2 parts; and water, 2 parts.
Prepare another solution of cupric sulphate, 1 part; water, 16 parts; and add ammonia until there is complete dissolution.

The metal is immersed in the first solution, then in the second solution in order to build a deposit of copper on the iron. The metal is then washed with water, after which it is immersed in a solution of sodium hyposulphite (with a few drops of hydrochloric acid added) and heated to 185° F. When the proper color is obtained, the metal is removed, dried, and polished.

f. Black:
Boil 1 part sulphur in 10 parts turpentine.
Brush a light coat over the metal, and heat the metal in the flame of an alcohol lamp to obtain the desired color.

g. Brown:
Wet the metal with a solution of iron perchloride, cupric sulphate, and nitric acid. Dry at 86° F. Steam over boiling water for 30 minutes, dry again at 86° F. Brush with a wire brush. Repeat the treatment until the proper color is achieved.

h. Brown:
Immerse the metal in a hot solution of nitric acid, 1 part; sweet spirits of nitre, 1 part; copper sulphate, 4 parts; tincturn muriatic iron, 2 parts; water, 60 parts.

i. Brown:
Clean the metal with a paste of whiting and soda, then immerse in a bath of dilute sulphuric acid, and rub with fine pumice powder. Expose the metal to the vapor of a mixture of 1 part concentrated hydrochloric acid and 1 part concentrated nitric acid. Heat the metal to 600° F., until a bronze color appears. When cool, coat with Vaseline, and reheat until the Vaseline begins to break down. Repeat the operation until the desired shade is obtained. (By adding acetic acid to the mixture of acids, yellow can be added to the metal in amounts in proportion to the amount of acetic acid in the solution.)

Tin — to Color Black

Immerse the metal in a solution of copper chloride, 8 ounces; antimony chloride, 3 ounces; and water (hot), 2 quarts.

Lead — to Color Black

Immerse the object in a solution of hydrochloric acid, 4 parts by weight; and water, 1 part.

Aluminum — to Color Black

a. Immerse the metal in a hot solution of zinc chloride, 1 pound; copper sulphate, 1.5 ounces; and water, 2 quarts.

b. Dissolve 1 ounce white arsenic, and 1 ounce sulphate of iron in 12 ounces hydrochloric acid. Add water, and immerse the freshly sanded aluminum. Dry in sawdust, and lacquer.

c. Polish the metal with fine emery paper; brush on a thin coat of olive oil; heat slowly over an alcohol flame. Repeat the treatment until the desired color is obtained. Polish with wool or leather.

d. Prepare a solution of sodium hydroxide, 4 ounces; calcium chloride, 1 ounce; and water, 1 quart. Dissolve the sodium hydroxide in water, and heat to 200° F. Dissolve the calcium chloride in the solution. Immerse the metal for 10-20 minutes. Remove. Dip the metal into the following solution for a few seconds: hydrochloric acid, 1 quart; white arsenic, 4 ounces; iron sulphate, 4 ounces; and water, 1 quart. Dry in sawdust; polish with an oily cloth.

e. Treat the aluminum with a commercial gun blue compounded for aluminum parts of guns, cameras, etc.

Aluminum — to Dye

Clean the aluminum in a bath of hot hydrogen potassium hydroxide; rinse in hot, then cold, water. Suspend the metal in lead tanks of sulphuric acid, applying high amperage and low voltage for 20-30 minutes at 28° F. to 31° F. Rinse; then dye by immersion in acid colors at 75° F., for 1 to 5 minutes. Seal by immersing in a bath of boiling acetic acid.

Copper, to Color

a. Steel gray:

Immerse the metal in a boiling solution of water, 1 pint; and arsenic chloride, 1 drachm.

b. Various colors:

Immerse the metal in a boiling solution of water, 1 quart; lead acetate, 300 grains; and sodium hyposulphite, 600 grains.

c. Steel gray:

Immerse the metal in a hot solution of muriate of arsenic, 4 ounces; and water, 2 quarts.

d. Red:

Immerse object in a hot solution of water, 1 pint; arsenic sulphide, 2 drachms; and potassium carbonate, 1 ounce.

e. Brown:

(Use hot)		
red lead oxide	59.9	parts by weight
chalk	12.0	parts by weight
acetic acid (glacial)	3.0	parts by weight
alcohol	6.0	parts by weight
water	19.1	parts by weight

f. Brown:

(Use hot)		
water	1	pint
iron nitrate	5	drachms

g. Brown:

(Use hot)		
acetic acid (6 %)	1.5	pints
potassium oxalate	1	ounce
ammonium chloride	3	ounces

h. Dark Brown:

(Use hot)		
water	1	pint
copper sulphate	1	ounce
sodium hyposulphate	1	ounce
hydrochloric acid	2	drachms

i. Antique:

potassium sulphide	1	cubic inch
water	1	pint
ammonia	6	drops

j. Orange:

Immerse the metal in a hot solution of crystallized copper acetate.

k. Violet:

Immerse the metal in a hot solution of antimony chloride; when dry, rub with cotton.

Brass — to Color

a. Red:

Immerse in solution of copper sulphate	5 ounces
potassium permanganate	7 ounces
water	500 ounces

b. Red to blue to lilac:

arsenic trisulphide	75 grains
sodium carbonate	150 grains
water	10 ounces

c. Fire red:

Immerse in a solution of potassium chlorate	75 grains
nickel carbonate	30 grains
salt of nickel	75 grains
water	16 ounces

d. Blue:

Immerse in solution of potassium sulphide	2 ounces
sodium chlorate	2 ounces
water	1,000 ounces

e. Blue:

Use hot solution of sodium thiosulphate	4 ounces
lead acetate	2 ounces
water	1 quart

f. Green:

Use hot solution of potassium bitartrate	24 grains
sodium chloride	48 grains
ammonium chloride	8 grains
copper nitrate	1 ounce
water	6 fluid ounces

g. Green:

Use hot solution of copper sulphate	120 grains
ammonium hydrochlorate	30 grains
water	1 quart

h. Brown:

iron nitrate	18 ounces
sodium thiosulphate	18 ounces
water	1 gallon

i. Brown to orange:

potassium chlorate	150 grains
copper sulphate	150 grains
water	1 quart

j. Red to blue:
    copper sulphate   32 drachms
    sodium hyposulphate   14 drachms
    potassium bitartrate   12 drachms
    water   1 quart

k. Fire red:
    potassium chlorate   30 drachms
    nickel carbonate   10 drachms
    salt of nickel   30 drachms
    water   32 ounces

l. Dark brown:
    potassium chlorate   30 drachms
    salt of nickel   60 drachms
    water   20 ounces

Bronze to Color

a. Green:
    Use hot solution of ammonium chloride   1 part
                        potassium bitartrate   3 parts
                        sodium chloride   3 parts
                        water   10 parts
                        add to the boiling solution   8 parts copper nitrate solution

b. Blue-green:
    Apply boiling solution of sodium thiosulphate   1 ounce
                              iron nitrate   8 ounces
                              water   1 gallon

c. Green:
    ammonium chloride   7 parts
    copper acetate   4 parts
    water   6 parts (by weight)

d. Dark green to black
    Use hot solution of potassium sulphide   1.5 ounces
                        sodium hydroxide   2.5 ounces
                        water   1 gallon

    Immerse the metal in this solution; remove; then paint on the following solution:
                    copper nitrate   8 ounces
                    ammonium chloride   4 ounces
                    acetic acid (6%)   4 fluid ounces
                    chromic acid   1 fluid ounce
                    water   1 gallon
                    Repeat when dry.

e. Blue-black:
    ammonium sulphide   2 ounces
    water   1 quart

f. Brown:
    Use hot solution of ammonium chloride   4 parts
                        potassium oxalate   1 part
                        acetic acid 5%   200 parts
    Treat and dry; repeat treatment; dry and brush.

To Electroplate Plaster (Copper)

Coat the plaster with shellac, spar varnish, or wax. Apply a coating of plumbago (powdered graphite); polish. Prepare a solution as follows:

Add 1/2 ounce of hydrochloric acid to each quart of water, then suspend a bag containing 1/2 pound of copper sulphate in the solution until it is saturated with copper sulphate.

Suspend a copper plate at the positive terminal, hanging clear in the solution. Immerse the treated plaster or object to be plated in the solution, and connect it to the negative terminal. Use low voltage (1-16 volts) and 6-8 amperes per square foot of surface to be plated.

Amperes required to plate 1-square-foot area

Nickel	4	amperes
Brass	6 - 8	amperes
Bronze	6 - 8	amperes
Copper	6 - 8	amperes
Silver	2	amperes
Gold	1.5	amperes
Zinc	10	amperes

Current must be D/C (direct current), and can be supplied by one or two automobile generators (in parallel) driven by a 1/4 h.p. electric motor.

Plating Solutions

a. Silver:

silver cyanide	4 parts by weight
potassium cyanide	10 parts by weight
water (distilled)	70 parts by weight

Use pure silver at the positive terminal.

b. Brass:

copper sulphate	1 part by weight
zinc sulphate	10 parts by weight
potassium cyanide	16 parts by weight
water (distilled)	1024 parts by weight

Use brass at the positive terminal.

c. Copper:

copper acetate	20 parts by weight
sodium carbonate	17 parts by weight
potassium cyanide	20 parts by weight
sodium sulphite	25 parts by weight
water (distilled)	1024 parts by weight

Use pure copper at the positive terminal.

d. Nickel:

nickel sulphate	10 parts by weight
sodium citrate	9 parts by weight
water (distilled)	288 parts by weight

Use pure nickel at the positive terminal.

Ivory and Bone — to Clean and Bleach

a. Wash with soap and warm water.

b. To bleach make a paste of fine damp sawdust. Saturate the paste with the juice of 2 lemons. Pack the ivory in the sawdust, and brush it away after it has dried.

c. Wash in mildly hot solution (by weight) of 1 part sodium bicarbonate to 10 parts water.

d. To bleach away yellow due to age. Suspend the material a few inches above a container of lime chloride moistened with hydrochloric acid. Cover with a glass, and expose to direct sunlight. Remove and wash the object with a solution of sodium bicarbonate, then rinse in clear water and dry. (Brittle ivory or bone can be rendered more flexible by soaking them for a short time in dilute phosphoric acid.)

Ivory — to Soften and Make Elastic

Ivory can be softened and made elastic by soaking the material in pure phosphoric acid until it loses some of its opacity. Then the ivory is washed in cold water and dried. Eventually it will again harden, but it can be softened again by soaking the material in hot water.

Ivory — to Harden

To harden ivory that has been softened by the above method, heat table salt (without burning) until it looses its crystalline appearance; then wrap the ivory in sheet of white writing paper, and cover it with the salt for at least 24 hours.

Ivory — to Etch

Paint the ivory with varnish or shellac, and scratch away the design to be etched. Apply a solution of 1 part sulphuric acid and 6 parts water. The etched lines will turn black. To obtain brown lines, dissolve 1 part silver nitrate in 5 parts water, and etch for a short time. Expose etched areas to the light until they turn brown.

Ivory — to Color

a. Black:
Wash in potassium hydroxide; then immerse in silver nitrate solution. Drain off the solution, and place in direct sunlight.

b. Red:
Soak in a solution of water   1,000 parts
                        acetic acid   100 parts
                        aniline red   5 parts
(Soak 24 hours; then dry and polish.)

c. Yellow:
Soak in a solution of lead acetate, rinse, and dry; then immerse in a solution of potassium chromate.

SOURCE LIST

The numbers following the items refer to the identifying numbers on the accompanying list of firms.

Air compressors 13, 19, 23, 34
Alabaster, 24
Aluminum, 16, 48, 73
Aluminum wire, 80
Aniline dye, 31
Barium carbonate, 26, 59
Beeswax, 12, 31, 75, 79, 80, 84
Blacksmith tools, 32, 50, 75
Brass, 16, 32, 33, 48, 58, 73
Brass shim, 28, 56, 57, 81
Brick dust (grog), 4, 26, 35, 59
Bronze, 32, 48, 73
Carnauba wax, 12, 55, 79, 84
Castable refractory material, 2
Casting materials, 6, 8, 29, 32, 38, 49, 71
Casting tools (sand), 32, 38, 55
Carborundum stones, 64, 75, 80
Ceramic materials, 1, 4, 26, 35, 37, 59
Ceramic shell materials, 53-85, 86
Chemicals, 12, 47
Clay preparation machinery, 22, 30, 51, 72
Clay (red), 4, 19, 26, 35, 59
Clay (stoneware), 19, 26, 35, 78
Commercial bronze foundry, 9
Copper, 16, 48, 73, 80
Crucibles, 32, 38, 55, 75
Dry pigment, 14, 31, 68, 79, 82
Electric power tools, 16, 25, 32, 61, 80, 81
Electroplating materials, 75
Emery stone, 64

LIST OF FIRMS

1. A. D. Alpine Co., 11837 Teale St., Culver City, Calif.
2. A. P. Green Fire Brick Co., Mexico, Missouri
3. Albert Constantine and Son, Inc., 2050 Eastehider Rd., Bronx, N.Y.
4. American Art Clay Co., 4717 W. 16th St., Indianapolis 24, Ind.
5. American Handicrafts Co., 193 William St., New York, N.Y.
6. American Smelting and Refining Co., 120 Broadway, New York, N.Y.
7. Arrow Tool Co., 1900 S. Costner Ave., Chicago 23, Ill.
8. Atlantic Chemicals and Metals Co., 1921-1927 N. Kenmore Ave., Chicago, Ill.
9. Avnet-Shaw, Commercial St., Engineers' Hill, Plainview, L.I., N.Y.
10. Bakelite Corp., 247 Park Ave., New York, N.Y.
11. Bedford Forge Co., 22 Interstate St., Bedford, Ohio
12. Behlen and Brothers Inc., 10 Christopher St., New York 14, N.Y.
13. Binks Mfg., Chicago 12, Ill.
14. Binney and Smith, 41 E. 42nd St., New York, N.Y.
15. Bloomington Limestone Corp., 110 E. 42nd St., New York 14, N.Y.

16. Brodhead Garrett Co., Cleveland, Ohio
17. Cadillac Plastic and Chemical Co., 15111 Second Ave., Detroit, Mich.
18. Can Pro Corp., Fond Du Lac, Wis.
19. Cedar Heights Clay Co., Oak Hill, Ohio
20. Craft Service, 360 University Ave., Rochester, N.Y.
21. Craftools, Inc., 396 Broadway, New York 13, N.Y.
22. Crossley Machine Co., Trenton, N.J.
23. DeVilbiss Co., Toledo 1, Ohio
24. Del-Glo Co., Box 930, Cheyenne, Wyo.
25. Delta Milwaukee Industrial Machine Tools, Rockwell Mfg. Co., Milwaukee 1, Wis.
26. Denver Fire Clay Co., P.O. Box 5510, Denver 17, Colo.
27. Du Pont de Nemours, E. I., and Co., Arlington, N.J.
28. Ettl Studios, 213 W. 58th St., New York 19, N.Y.
29. Fenton Foundry Supply, 134 Gilbert Ave., Dayton, Ohio
30. Fernholtz Machine Co., 8468 Melrose Place, Los Angeles 46, Calif.
31. Fezandie and Sperrle, Inc., 102 Lafayette St., New York 13, N.Y.
32. Freeman Supply Co., 1152 E. Broadway, Toledo 5, Ohio
33. Fulton Metallurgical Products Corp., 4710 Ellsworth Ave., Pittsburgh 13, Pa.
34. Gardner-Denver Co., Quincy, Ill.
35. George Fetzer, 1205 17th Ave., Columbus 11, Ohio
36. Granite City Tool Co., Barre, Vermont
37. H. C. Spinks Clay Co., 1103 First National Bank Building, Cincinnati 2, Ohio
38. Hill and Griffith Co., Birmingham 1, Ala.
39. Indian Hill Stone Co., Bloomington, Ind.
40. Indiana Limestone Co., 40 E. 41st St., New York 17, N.Y.
41. J. H. Monteath Co., 2500 Park Ave., Bronx 51, N.Y.
42. Johnson Gas Appliance Co., Cedar Rapids, Iowa
43. Marblette Corp., 37-21 30th St., Long Island City 1, N.Y.
44. Master Power Corp., 6225 Cochran Road, Solon 39, Ohio
45. McEnglevan Speedy-Melt Div., P.O. Box 31, 708 Griggs St., Danville, Ill.
46. Mobile Oil Co., Hanna Bldg., Cleveland, Ohio
47. Monsanto Chemical Co., Springfield, Mass.
48. Pacific Metals Co., 3100 19th St., San Francisco, Calif.
49. Peerless Mineral Products Co., Conneaut, Ohio

50. Perma-flex Mold Co., 1919 E. Livingston Ave., Columbus 9, Ohio
51. Perry Equipment Corp., 1421 North 6th St., Philadelphia 22, Pa.
52. Pittsburgh Plate Glass Co., Grant Bldg., Pittsburgh 19, Pa.
53. Pre-Vest, Inc., 23420 Lakeland Blvd., Cleveland 23, Ohio
54. Rohm and Haas Co., Philadelphia 5, Pa.
55. Saunders Alexander and Co., 28 Chestnut St. P.O. Box 265, Cold Spring-on-Hudson, N. Y.
56. Sculpture Associates, 101 St. Marks Place, 9, N.Y.
57. Sculpture House, 38 E. 30th St., New York 16, N.Y.
58. Seeger Brass Co., 23 St. Clair, Toledo, Ohio
59. Standard Ceramics Supply Co., 1466 River Ave., Pittsburgh 12, Pa.
60. Standard Equipment, 3175 Fulton St., Brooklyn 8, N.Y.
61. The Stellhorn Co., 300 S. Summit St., Toledo, Ohio
62. Studio Supply Co., 23 Judge St., Brooklyn 11, N.Y.
63. Trani Marble and Tile Works, 437 E. 23rd St., New York 10, N.Y.
64. Trow and Holden Co., Barre, Vermont
65. Tuscora Foundry Sand Co., Canal Fulton, Ohio
66. U.S. Gypsum Co., 300 W. Adams St., Chicago 6, Ill.
67. U.S. Industrial Tool and Supply Co., 13541 Auburn, Detroit, Mich.
68. Utrech Linen, 3303 5th St., Brooklyn, N. Y.
69. Vermarco Supply Co., 3321 Prospect Ave., Cleveland 15, Ohio
70. Vermont Marble Co., 101 Park Ave., New York 17, N.Y.
71. Warwick Industrial Furnace and Engineering Corp., 452 W. Chicago Ave., Chicago 10, Ill.
72. Walker Jamar Co., 365 South First Ave. East, Duluth 2, Minn.
73. Whitehead Metal Products Co., 303 W. 10th St., New York 11, N.Y.
74. Whiting Corp., Harvey, Ill.
75. Wm. Dixon, Inc., 34-42 Inney St., Newark, N. J.
76. The Woodshed, 105½ St. Marks Place, New York 9, N.Y.
77. X-Acto, Inc., 48-41 Van Dam St., Long Island, 1, N. Y.
78. Zanesville Stoneware Co., Zanesville, Ohio
79. Local paint stores
80. Local hardware stores
81. Local auto parts houses
82. Local builders' supply
83. Local marine supply
84. Local drug stores

85. Nalco Chemical Company, Metal Industries Division, 9165 South Harbor Ave., Chicago, Illinois 60617
86. The Ransom & Randolf Company, 324 Chestnut, Toledo, Ohio

BIBLIOGRAPHY*

BATTEN, MARK, *Stone Sculpture by Direct Carving.* The Studio Publications, London, 1957.

BLUM and HOGABOOM, *Principles of Electroplating and Electroforming*, McGraw-Hill Book Company, New York, 1950.

CAMPBELL, HARRY L., *Metal Castings*, John Wiley & Sons, Inc., New York, 1936.

CHASE and POST, *A History of Sculpture*, Harper and Brothers Publishers, New York, 1925.

ELLENBERGER, BAUM, and DITTRICH, *An Atlas of Animal Anatonmy for Artists*, Dover Publications, Inc., New York, 1956.

HOFFMAN, MALVINA, *Sculpture Inside and Out*, Bonanza Books, New York, 1939.

HOLTROP and HJORTH, *Principles of Woodworking*, The Bruce Publishing Company, Milwaukee, Wis., 1961.

KEPES, GYORGY, *The Language of Vision*, Paul Theobald and Co., Chicago, 1951.

MAYER, RALPH, *The Artist's Handbook of Materials and Techniques*, The Viking Press, New York, 1957.

---

*References listed alphabetically by author surname where possible; volumes not so listed appear — alphabetically by book title — at the conclusion of the Bibliography.

MINER and MILLER, *Exploring Patternmaking and Foundry*, D. Van Nostrand Company, Inc., Princeton, N. J., 1964.

MOHOLY-NAGY, L., *Vision in Motion*, Paul Theobald, Chicago, 1947.

NELSON, GLEN C., *Ceramics*, Holt, Rinehart and Winston, Inc., New York, 1960.

NEUMANN, ROBERT, VON, *The Design and Creation of Jewelry*, Chilton Co., Philadelphia, 1961.

READ, HERBERT, *A Concise History of Modern Sculpture*, Frederick A. Praeger, Publisher, New York, 1964.

RHODES, DANIEL, *Clay and Glazes for the Potter*, Greenberg Publishers, New York, 1957.

RICH, JACK, *The Materials and Methods of Sculpture*, Oxford University Press, Inc., New York, 1947.

RITCHIE, ANDREW C., *Sculpture of the Twentieth Century*, The Museum of Modern Art, New York.

ROOD, JOHN, *Sculpture in Wood*, University of Minnesota Press, Minneapolis, Minn., 1950.

ROYCE, JOSEPH, *Surface Anatomy*, F. A. Davis Co., Philadelphia, 1965.

SCHIDER, FRITZ, *An Atlas of Anatomy for Artists*, Dover Publications, New York, 1957.

SEUPHOR, MICHEL, *The Sculpture of This Century*, George Braziller, Inc., New York, 1961.

STRUPPECK, JULES, *The Creation of Sculpture*, Henry Holt and Co., New York, 1952.

ZORACH, WILLIAM, *Zorach Explains Sculpture*, American Artists Group, New York, 1947.

Dictionary of Modern Sculpture, Robert Maillard, (Ed.), Tudor Publishing Company, New York, 1960.

How To Use Castolite Liquid Plastics and Fiberglass, Castolite Company, Woodstock, Illinois, 1959.

Modern Plastics Encyclopedia, Hildreth Press Inc., Bristol, Conn., 1963.

The Oxy-Acetylene Handbook, Line Air Products Co., New York, 1954.

Vasari on Technique, L. S. Machelhose (Tr.), New York, 1907.

GLOSSARY OF TERMS

ABSTRACT — The simplification or generalization of forms usually found in nature, sometimes to the extent that they become unrecognizable.

ABSTRACT TEXTURES — The simplification and rearrangement of existing tactile qualities.

ACADEMIC — Traditional; conforming to an established order, usually sacrificing originality and expression.

AGGREGATE — Inactive substances added to cohesive or adhesive materials, often for the purposes of increasing strength or bulk.

ALLOY — A metal formed by the fusion of two or more metals to obtain physical characteristics unlike either of the original metals.

ANNEAL — The controlled heating and cooling of metal to alleviate internal stress which causes fracturing.

ASYMMETRIC BALANCE — Balance which occurs through the manipulation of unlikes.

AUTOGRAPHIC — Being so sensitive that every impression is recorded, as a finger print on clay.

BALANCE — A state of equilibrium.

BAT — A plaster slab used to absorb excess moisture from clay.

BEAD — The line formed by a continuous weld, usually along a seam.

BINDER — A material which causes a state of cohesion.

BISQUE WARE — The first heating of unglazed clay which turns the ware into a hard, consolidated mass.

BLUNGE — To mix, forming a liquid suspension.

BRAZE — To join metals using heat and a foreign metal as a binding agent.

BURN-OUT — The heating of a flask in order to drive out water and other volatile materials, especially wax.

BUCKSAW — A sawblade fixed in a frame and used by one person to cut wood.

CAMEO — Relief carving in which the image stands above the background.

CARBORUNDUM SLIP — A thin sharpening stone made of silicon carbide.

CARVER'S DRILL — A plug drill; a drill that depends on impact rather than rotary cutting motion to cut holes in stone.

CAST — To reproduce a given shape by pouring a temporarily fluid material into a mold. The solidified material is the reproduction.

CENTRIFUGAL — Outward force exerted on a body moving in a curving (circular) path.

CERAMIC — Referring to all which is related to the consolidation of silicates of aluminum through heat of fusion, including glass and clay.

CHARGE — To load, as to load a furnace or crucible.

COLOR — 1. A general term for the character of light; includes hue, value, and intensity. 2. A term used in sculpture to describe the shading on a three-dimensional surface.

CONE — A device used to measure the heat work of a kiln.

CONTENT — The meaning or significance of a work of art which is a product of Form, and evidenced in aesthetic experience.

CONTOUR — The outer edge of a shape when viewed from any given position.

CRUCIBLE — A container made of refractory material or metal and used to heat substances to high temperatures.

DECANT — To remove liquid which forms at the top of a mixture as the solids settle.

DISTORT — To deviate from the normal shape of an object.

DISTORTION — A condition of all works of art which occurs through interpretation or conception by an artist and which results in exaggeration.

DRAFT — An angle or taper frequently given to pattern edges in order to enable the pattern to be drawn from a mold without causing injury to the mold; a shallow groove.

DROSS — A waste product taken off of molten metal during melting in the form of scum (a granular oxide).

EDGE — A condition which exists when planes intersect, or at the contour of an object, and usually interpreted as a drawn line in the graphic arts.

ELABORATION — To add details or to give more extensive treatment.

EMERY STONE — A stone of considerable hardness, consisting of silicon carbide mixed with an oxide of iron, used for grinding or polishing.

ENGLISH HONE — A fine, dense sharpening stone.

EXCELSIOR — Stringy, curled wood-shaving used as a packing material.

EXPRESSIONISM — An art form based on emotional interpretation of the relationships of the elements.

FILTER PRESS — A machine which extracts excess water from slip clay through hydraulic, pneumatic, or mechanical pressure.

FIRE — To heat or burn objects in a controlled situation.

FLASK — A complete mold box, or an invested model.

FLUX — 1. Any substance used to aid fusion of metals. 2. A material which combines with surface impurities on metal, in effect cleaning the metal.

FORGE — 1. A furnace used to heat metal. 2. To shape metal through heat and impact.

FORM — Unity or order which can be achieved in the use of the elements of sculpture.

FREE STANDING — Sculpture which is designed to be seen from all sides including the top and which usually supports itself and is not part of, or attached to, a wall or background.

FUNCTION — To serve.

GALVANIZED IRON — Iron which is coated with zinc to prevent rust.

GATE — A system of openings or channels in a mold through which molten metal is poured in order to fill a mold cavity.

GESSO — A heavy fluid used as a base coat for paint, traditionally made of plaster of Paris and glue, but more recently of white pigment and a synthetic binder.

GLAZE — A heat-created vitreous glass surface, a covering for ceramic ware.

GLYPTIC — Retaining the visual quality of a material and the basic geometric nature of the mass.

GRAPHIC — Two-dimensional art forms, i.e., painting, drawing, and printmaking.

GREENWARE — Finished clay ware that is dry but has not been heated into a homogenous mass.

GROG — Burned, crushed clay that is added to plastic clay.

HARMONY — Agreement or accord; orderly.

HELIARC — An electric welding machine that surrounds the area of the weld with inert gas to prevent oxidization of the metal in the weld.

HONE — To sharpen a cutting edge to its finest edge.

HUE — The term which describes specific wave lengths of light, such as red, yellow, or blue.

HYPOTHESIS — An assertion or assumption.

IDEALIZED — To represent in an ultimate character; a state of perfection beyond possibility.

ILLUSIONISTIC — To misrepresent a medium to the extent that images created through the medium appear to be real.

IMPRESSIONISM — An art form based on the interpretation of visual sensation.

INTAGLIO RELIEF — Sculpture in which the surface of the image is below the surface of the background.

INTRINSIC — Belonging to the essential nature of a thing.

INVESTMENT — A refractory material used in the making of molds for the casting of metals.

KERF — A groove; the space left by a saw blade during a cut, and equal to the width of the blade across the teeth.

LADLE — A container for dipping and pouring metal, usually made of iron.

LAMINATE — A thickness built up of layers of material, usually glued together.

LAPIDARY — Pertaining to the art of cutting stones.

LATEX — Formerly raw rubber; now any rubber-like plastic mass.

LAW OF FRONTALITY — A position in sculpture in which a figure faces forward, rigid, without twist to the body.

LIGNUM VITAE — A heavy hardwood ranging in color from orange to dark brown.

LINEAR — Involving or consisting of lines; looking like a line, narrow or elongated.

LUTO — Used investment which has been crushed to be used again.

MALLEABLE — Capable of being extended or shaped by impact or pressure.

MASS — A body of apparently coherent matter.

MATRIX — A material that gives foundation to something embodied or enclosed in it.

MEDIA — The materials used by the artist.

MEDIUM — Singular form of *media*.

MOBILITY — Movable, the state or quality of being movable.

MODEL — 1. To shape by pressure. 2. A master or mother shape.

MOLD — 1. A shell containing a reverse image of a model or master which serves as a shaping container when filled with a temporarily liquid ma-terial and which becomes the casting when it has hardened. 2. To shape by pressure.

MONOLITHIC — A mass which is solid, not composed of smaller units.

MONUMENTALITY — A condition of sculpture in which it has the quality of hugeness or massiveness, regardless of actual size — often with the result that the object appears to be larger than it is.

MUFFLE — A furnace designed so that its contents are protected from direct contact with flame.

MULLER — A machine which uses large rollers to condition clay through a smashing action.

NATURAL TEXTURE — A texture resulting from nature, not man-made.

NATURALISM — Imagery as close to nature as possible, without editorializing by the artist.

NONFERROUS — Metals other than iron.

OPAQUE — Not transparent; without the ability to transmit light.

ORIENTATION — Acquaintance with an existing environment, or the establishment of a fixed direction.

OXIDIZING FLAME — A flame with an excess of oxygen.

PARTING — A powder without binding qualities used to separate layers of sand in a sand mold.

PATINA — Originally, the natural color of oxidized metal surfaces; more recently, the surface coloring given to various materials such as metal, wood, and plaster when used in relation to sculpture.

PERSPECTIVE — The systematic depiction on a flat surface of the illusion of consistent depth.

PICKLE — An acid bath used to remove burnt sand, scale, or specific impurities from the surface of metal.

PIECE MOLD — A mold constructed in sections so that it can be used repeatedly.

PIGMENT — A minute particle, which reflects a specific hue, used in the formation of paint or ink.

PITCH — A residue from the distillation of tar and petroleum.

PLANE — A curved or flat continuous surface defined by edges.

PLASTIC — 1. A material malleable enough to be manipulated by hand. 2. A synthetic coherent material.

PLUMB BOB — A weight on a string used to indicate vertical direction.

POT METAL — White metal, i.e., lead, tin, and cadmium-based metals.

PROPORTION — Size relationship of part to part, often in comparison to forms found in nature.

PROPORTIONAL DIVIDERS — A measuring tool which mechanically adjusts size ratios.

PUG MILL — A machine, similar to a meat grinder, which prepares plastic clay.

PUMICE STONE — A porous volcanic glass used in polishing.

PUTTY POWDER — A crude stannic acid powder used for fine polishing.

QUENCH — To cool heated metal by immersion in a liquid.

RAKE — Slant or slope.

REALISTIC — Pertaining to general appearances as found in nature.

REDUCING FLAME — A flame with insufficient oxygen to support complete combustion.

REFRACTORY — A material which resists the action of heat.

RELIEF — An art form which is graphic in concept, but utilizes shallow depth (projection) to establish images.

REPOUSSE — A relief in which the image is produced primarily by impact on the back of the medium, usually soft sheet metal.

RESIN — Certain solid or semisolid organic or synthetic substances with significant binding qualities.

RETAINING SHELL — An outside casing used to hold a piece mold together.

RHYTHM — A continuous measured sequence of similar or equal units.

RIDDLE — 1. A screen (sieve) used to sift casting sand. 2. To sift casting sand onto a model from considerable height.

RISER — A space in a mold above the cavity that is used to supply liquid metal to thick sections of a casting that may shrink during cooling.

RUNNER — A channel in a mold which feeds metal from the sprue to the cavity.

SCRAPER — A tool which cuts with a dragging action.

SCRIBE (metal) — A hard, pointed metal tool (sometimes tipped with a diamond) used to draw on metal.

SHAPE — Closed, definable area.

SHARPENING SLIP — A small abrasive stone used for putting a cutting edge on tools.

SICCATIVE — A binding material used to give a clay body added adhesion.

SIMULATED TEXTURE — A tactile quality which has been copied.

SLAKE — To soak in water.

SLIP — A thin, runny suspension of clay in water.

SLURRY — A watery mud-like substance.

SOLDER — To bond metals using heat to melt in the joint between them, low temperature alloys of lead which adhere to the two adjoining metal surfaces.

SPACE — 1. A three-dimensional expanse. 2. The interval between objects.

SPALLS — Fragments, chips, or splinters, usually related to stone.

SPRUE — A channel or opening in a mold which conveys molten metal to the runners, and the metal which solidifies in the channel.

STAKE — Shaped metal tool which fits into a square hole on an anvil or similar base, and which serves as an extension of the anvil, for the creation of selective shapes through impact.

STAMPS — Textured objects which are used to impress textures or designs in clay, wood, leather, metal, and so on.

SUBJECT MATTER — The theme or story often associated with a work of art.

SUBORDINATE — Of secondary importance.

SYMMETRICAL — Divisible into identical parts by passing a plane through the center. (Commonly, in graphic forms, the plane is passed vertically through the forms.)

SYNCOPATION — Accenting rhythmic patterns in an unexpected way, usually to create interest.

TACTILE — Pertaining to the sense of touch.

TAMP — To force by impact; to stamp.

TEMPER — The degree of hardness or elasticity acquired by metals after being subjected to controlled heating and cooling.

TENSILE — Relating to the ability of a material to be stretched or drawn.

TENSION — A state of strain, stress, or excitement resulting from form or position.

TERRAZZO — A polish conglomerate consisting of cement and colored stones.

TEXTURE — The surface quality of any material which can be sensed, or appear to be sensed, by touch; having tactile qualities.

THERMOPLASTIC — Material which becomes pliable with the application of heat, while maintaining other inherent characteristics.

THERMOWELDING — A method of joining materials with heat; usually refers to the bonding of plastic with jets of hot gas or by passing the plastic between hot rollers.

THREE-DIMENSIONAL — Physically measurable in a constant scale, on three axes — length, height, and depth.

TIME — A system indicating duration, measured by a consistent sequence of events not occurring simultaneously.

TORQUE — The result of forces applied in such a way as to cause twist or rotation.

TOTALITY — The state of being whole or complete.

TRANSPARENT — Allowing the passage of light without significantly obscuring the image.

Twist drill — A drill having a round shank and spiral fluting.

Value — The comparative quantity of light reflected, appearing to range from light to dark or black to white, and related to shading.

Vent — A passage in a mold designed to exhaust gasses incurred during the casting of metal.

Void — An empty space; a negative area.

Volatile — Having the ability to readily pass into a gaseous state.

Volume — Three-dimensional quantity, often easily measurable; in sculpture, usually rigid.

Waste mold — A mold which must be destroyed to release a casting.

Wedge — To mix plastic clay by cutting and squeezing.

Weld — To fuse; to join like metals by melting the metal along the bond line so that molten metals flow together forming one unit, sometimes with the addition of a filler metal.

INDEX

All references to figures appear in bold face.